TOKYO

|CONDENSED|

 John Ashburne

LONELY PLANET PUBLICATIONS
Melbourne • Oakland • London • Paris

contents

Tokyo Condensed
1st edition – February 2002

Published by
Lonely Planet Publications Pty Ltd
ABN 36 005 607 983
90 Maribyrnong St, Footscray, Vic 3011, Australia
www.lonelyplanet.com or AOL keyword: lp

Lonely Planet offices
Australia Locked Bag 1, Footscray, Vic 3011
☎ 613 8379 8000 fax 613 8379 8111
e| talk2us@lonelyplanet.com.au
USA   150 Linden St, Oakland, CA 94607
☎ 510 893 8555 Toll Free: 800 275 8555
fax 510 893 8572
e| info@lonelyplanet.com
UK   10a Spring Place, London NW5 3BH
☎ 020 7428 4800 fax 020 7428 4828
e| go@lonelyplanet.co.uk
France   1 rue du Dahomey, 75011 Paris
☎ 01 55 25 33 00 fax 01 55 25 33 01
e| bip@lonelyplanet.fr
www.lonelyplanet.fr

Design Jenny Jones Maps Charles Rawlings-Way
Editing Victoria Harrison and George Dunford Cover
Maria Vallianos Publishing Manager Diana Saad
Thanks to Alison Lyall, Annie Horner, Bibiana Jaramillo,
Brett Pascoe, Gabrielle Green, Gerard Walker, GIS Unit,
Kerrie Williams, Quentin Frayne, Tim Fitzgerald and extra
big arigatos to Trent Paton.

Photographs
Many of the images in this guide are available for
licensing from Lonely Planet Images.
e| lpi@lonelyplanet.com.au;
www.lonelyplanetimages.com
Images also used with kind permission of Tokyo
National Museum; Sapporo Breweries, Ltd.

Front cover photographs
Top: Rainbow Bridge
(John McInnes)
Bottom: sign from JR Yamanote train
(Martin Moos)

ISBN 1 74059 069 4

Text & maps © Lonely Planet Publications 2002
Tokyo Subway System Map © March 2001 TRTA
Photos © photographers as indicated 2002
Printed through Colorcraft Ltd., Hong Kong
Printed in China

how to use this book

SYMBOLS

- ⊠ address
- ☎ telephone number
- ⊖ nearest subway station
- ⊠ nearest train station
- ⊟ nearest bus route
- 🚗 auto route, parking details
- ⊘ opening hours
- ⓘ tourist information
- ⑤ cost, entry charge
- 🄴 email/website address
- ♿ wheelchair access
- ⚢ child-friendly
- ✗ on-site or nearby eatery
- ⩔ good vegetarian selection

COLOUR-CODING

Each chapter has a different colour code which is reflected on the maps for quick reference (eg all Highlights are bright yellow on the maps).

MAPS

The fold-out maps inside front and back covers are numbered from 1 to 13. All sights and venues in the text have map references which indicate where to find them on the maps; eg (2, C3) means Map 2, grid reference C3. Although each item is not pinpointed on the maps, the street address is always indicated.

PRICES

Price gradings (eg ¥1000/500) usually indicate adult/concession entry charges to a venue. Concession prices can include senior, student, member or coupon discounts.

AUTHOR AUTHOR !

John Ashburne

John ditched up in Tokyo, clueless, in 1985, where he took up semi-permanent residence on a park bench in the shadow of Tokyo Tower. It was, he confesses, a handy early morning stagger from Roppongi.

Sixteen years later he still resides in Japan, hopefully a bit less clueless, in Kyoto. He is compelled to make regular trips up to the Big Ume-boshi to check that Tokyo Tower is still bloody ugly, and the buckwheat noodles are still bloody sublime. He wishes to be reincarnated as an Asakusa rāmen shop owner.

Special thanks to Masami 'Gambaru' Itoh, Sasha, Yūko Takeyama & the friendly students of Musashino Arts University.

READER FEEDBACK

Things change – prices go up, schedules change, good places go bad and bad places improve or go bankrupt. So, if you find things better or worse, recently opened or long since closed, please tell us and help make the next edition even more accurate. Send all correspondence to the Lonely Planet office closest to you (listed on p. 2) or visit www.lonelyplanet.com/feedback.

Lonely Planet books provide independent advice. Lonely Planet does not accept advertising in guidebooks, nor payment in exchange for listing or endorsing any place or business. Lonely Planet writers do not accept discounts or payments in exchange for positive coverage of any sort.

facts about tokyo

Tokyo, like all great cities, is a conundrum, a riddle of contradictions that springs from tensions between large-scale ugliness and meticulous detail. It is a creative behemoth, inevitably reinventing, recreating, resolving itself. It is chaos at the centre. It's a meteoric speedball that doesn't give a shit. It may well be the perfect metaphor for the globe as it spins and wobbles off course into the 21st century and naturally, it's a lot of fun.

In Tokyo, Japan Incorporated rubs shoulders with the nation's closeted Imperial dynasty. World-class hotels, trendy boutiques and eateries crowd together with Buddhist temples. The world's biggest and most lavish department stores peer down on tiny specialist shops and restaurants. Mazes of narrow alleys blaze with neon by night. And in the shadow of the overhead expressways exist pockets of another Tokyo – an old wooden house, a *ryokan* inn, an old lady in *geta* slippers sweeping the pavement.

The contradictions jump out at you unexpectedly on a crowded street – the teenage girl dressed in kimono buying a hamburger at McDonald's or the Buddhist monk with an alms bowl, poised serenely in the midst of jostling shoppers in Ginza. Look closely. His shock-proof watch sports an altimeter. Tokyo is a living city. It is less a collection of sights than a total experience, the urban explorer's ultimate dream.

Night-time traffic in Tokyo's dazzling Ginza district

HISTORY
The Early Years

When the first European visitors, Portuguese traders, first set eyes on 16th-century Edo, it was little more than a festering swamp. Its chief tourist attraction was an abandoned castle, and frankly it stank of fish. Within three centuries, Edo would usurp Kyoto as Japan's traditional seat of imperial power. And Tokyo would be born.

Tokugawa Edo

The father to this upstart child was, undeniably, the mighty, wily, madly ambitious *shōgun* (top military administrator), Tokugawa Ieyasu. His appointment by the emperor, in 1603 was to change the fate of Tokyo (and Japan) forever.

Ieyasu was a political survivor. He knew he must 'divide and conquer' his political foes. In a masterstroke, he forced all *daimyō* (feudal lords) throughout Japan to spend at least one year out of every two in Edo (not least by forcibly incarcerating their wives and children within the city walls). This policy of dislocation made it difficult for ambitious *daimyō*.

Ieyasu had control. He systematically created a rigidly hierarchical society, comprising, in descending order: the nobility (in reality, powerless); the daimyō and their samurai; the farmers; and finally the artisans and merchants. Class dress, living quarters and even manner of speech were all strictly codified. Class advancement was prohibited. Though you could always, terrifyingly, go down to the underclasses, to the 'non-human' *hinin* and *eta*, the untouchable class.

Edo-period ukiyo-e : Hour of the Snake, *from the series* Women at various hours of the day *by Kitagawa Utamaro*

Tokyo National Museum

Isolation

After Ieyasu's death in 1616, his grandson Tokugawa Iemitsu, fearing Christian power, closed the country's borders in 1638. Japan was effectively removed from the world stage for nearly 300 years.

By the early 17th century, Edo (population over one million) was the largest city on earth. Its caste-like society divided the city into the daimyō's high city (Yamanote) and a low working-class city (Shitamachi). Destructive fires often swept through its shantytowns. The locals christened these *Edo no hana*, or 'flowers of Edo'. The cocky bravura of the expression sums up the tough Tokyo Shitamachi spirit. It's still to be found in the backstreets of Ueno and Asakusa.

Tokyo Rising

When Commodore Matthew Perry's armada of 'black ships' entered Edo (Tokyo) Bay demanding 'free trade' in 1853, despite spirited resistance from 2000 Tokugawa loyalists at the brief Battle of Ueno, the Shogunate fell apart. The Emperor upped sticks from Kyoto, and a new capital was born. Its name was Tokyo.

The Meiji Restoration refers to the consequent return of power to the Emperor. However Emperor Meiji's rule was more a revolution than a restoration. A crash course in

Tokyo National Museum

Actor Otani Oniji 3rd as the yakko Edobei *by Toshusai Sharaku, 1794*

industrialisation and militarisation began and by 1889 Japan had adopted a western-style constitution. And western-style empire-building. Nowhere was revolutionary change more evident than on the streets of the country's new capital city. Job seekers flocked from the country and Tokyo boomed.

Catastrophe & War

The Great Kantō Earthquake struck the boom town at noon on 1 September 1923. The subsequent fires, lasting some 40 hours, laid waste to the city. Some 142,000 lost their lives but worse was to come.

Uyoku – Far-out Right

Sinister black buses and vans occasionally prowl Tokyo's streets blaring out patriotic Japanese songs that sound like cheesey *anime* theme songs. These vehicles are the propaganda arm of the *uyoku,* a collection of far-right political organisations.

While initially alarming, uyoku pose no threat to tourists with their messages aimed at the Japanese public. Bus speakers issue out diatribes damning Japanese politicians or glorying in nationalist sentiment including the catchcry 'Revere the emperor! Expel the barbarian!'

Although most Japanese dismiss them as cranks, there is a dark side to the boys in red and black. Uyoku intimidate critics of the emperor with threats of violence, which are occasionally carried out.

A birds-eye view of the capital

John Hay

From the accession of Emperor Hirohito in 1926, nationalist fervour gripped the government. In 1931 the Japanese army invaded Manchuria, then China. By 1940 a pact with Germany and Italy had been signed and 'Greater Asia Co-Prosperity Sphere' was touted as the New Order. On 7 December 1941 the Japanese attacked Pearl Harbor.

WWII was catastrophic for Tokyo. Incendiary bombing of the mostly wooden city commenced in March 1944. On the nights of the 9th and 10th March 1945, 40% of the city was engulfed in a terrible firestorm and between 70,000 and 80,000 perished. Asakusa's Sensō-ji temple, and later the Meiji-jingū shrine were reduced to ashes.

By the time Emperor Hirohito made his famous address to the Japanese people on 15 August 1945, much of Tokyo was wasteland.

Boom & Gloom

Tokyo rose phoenix-like from the ashes of WWII. The economy boomed as almost no other had in history. Ironically, it was sparked by US involvement in the neighbouring Korean War. The 1960s, 70s and early 80s saw unprecedented growth. Japan was suddenly an economic superpower – incredibly wealthy, globally powerful, omnipotent.

And then it wasn't. The burst of the 80s bubble economy dealt Japan a financial blow from which it has yet to recover. But the cracks ran deeper than the fiscal fault-lines. In March 1995, when members of the Aum Shinrikyō cult released sarin nerve gas on a crowded Tokyo commuter train, killing 12 and injuring 5000, Japan's self-belief took a severe body blow. What will the future hold? The country looks to Tokyo for leadership, guidance. Yet Nagatachō remains deathly silent.

ORIENTATION

Tokyo is huge, but it's navigable. Though it doesn't posses one 'centre' as such, its cities-within-the-city are all easily accessible. You can be anywhere within an hour.

Here's a mental map. Imagine the London Tube symbol: a circle bisected across the middle by a single, straight line. The circle is the JR Yamanote line. On it, within it, or only just outside it, are all the major sights, attractions and business destinations.

The centre line, with a wee bit of geo-poetic license, consists of the overground Sōbu, and subway Chiyoda, Marunouchi, Ginza and Ōedo lines. At the centre of everything is the Imperial Palace. To the right along the line, lie Ginza and Marunouchi. Heading left of centre we pass Akasaka and Roppongi. Where the line hits the circle, is Shinjuku.

Following the Yamanote line, clockwise from here, we have: Shinjuku; Ikebukuro; Ueno; Asakusa (just off); Akihabara; Kanda; Tokyo; Yūrakuchō (and nearby Ginza); Shimbashi; Shinagawa; Meguro; Ebisu; Shibuya; Harajuku, then you're back at Shinjuku. Only Ōdaiba is out of the loop, at roughly 5.30 if the Yamanote was a clock face.

Japanese Addresses

In Tokyo finding a place from its address can be a near impossibility, even for the Japanese. The usual process is to ask directions (even taxi drivers often have to do this). Businesses often include a small map in their advertisements, cards and websites to show their location.

Apart from main roads, *dōri*, very few streets have names. Addresses work by narrowing down the location of a building to a number within an area of a few blocks. Unlike European addresses, they work from top to bottom. Thus, Tokyo would be indicated first, followed by the *ku* (ward), then the *chō* or *machi* (loosely, suburb) and then the *chōme*, which is an area of just a couple of blocks: eg *Chiyoda-ku, Nagatachō 2-10-3, Capitol Hotel, 3F.* The ground floor is always counted as the first.

Look for floor numbers (1F, 2F etc) amid the Japanese script on building exteriors. One good way to avoid getting lost is to refer to major landmarks. We've provided station and exit references for venues listed in this book.

Tokyo Metropolitan Expressway – 220km of it girds the city

John Hay

ENVIRONMENT

The events of the morning of 30 September 1999, sent shivers of fear through the city and the nation as Japan experienced its worst ever nuclear accident. The farcical elements of the tragedy – which occurred at the JCO nuclear power plant in Tokai-mura, Ibaragi, only 140 kilometres north of the capital – did nothing to allay serious questions about how the country's nuclear program is monitored and run. The ensuing nuclear chain reaction raged uncontrolled for around twenty hours leaving three workers dead, and Tokyoites understandably nervous about the fast-breeder reactor program the government is aggressively promoting, just on their doorsteps.

Guarding against flu, not radioactive fall-out.

In other environment-related areas, the government seems all too happy to pander to big business interests. Pollution-related cases from decades ago are still dragging through the courts. It seems the government prefers grey suits to green action. While recycling programs have been established by most local governments and enthusiastically adopted by local residents, there is still too much plastic packaging in use. The disposal of plastic is a major contribution to air pollution in Tokyo. Once again, the contradictions abound.

The Big One

Every Tokyo resident's worst fear – the next 'big one' – became an even more tangible threat on 17 January 1995, when Kōbe was devastated by an earthquake that measured 7.2 on the Richter scale. People began to wonder what would happen if a similar or stronger quake hit sprawling, densely populated Tokyo.

Though almost imperceptible earthquakes happen nearly every day, the last one to give Tokyo a major shakedown was the 1923 'Great Kantō Earthquake'. Although Tokyo is not the city it was in 1923, the prospect of another major earthquake remains a grim one. Earthquake prediction is hardly an exact science, and no-one is sure if Tokyo is overdue for a major quake or not.

The recent Kōbe earthquake was a reminder to the people of Tokyo and elsewhere in Japan that the mighty geological forces that created their islands are still at work. And the devastation in central Kōbe reminded them that no amount of earthquake preparation is too much.

Residents of Tokyo are used to frequent small earthquakes that cause no damage. There's no point in being paranoid, but it is worth checking emergency exits in your hotel and being aware of earthquake safety procedures. These include turning off anything that might cause a fire, opening a door or window to secure an exit and sheltering in a doorway or under a sturdy table when tremors begin.

GOVERNMENT & POLITICS

Sleaze, corruption, rightists in-bed-with-the-Mafia, authors-turning-politicos, politicos-turning-authors, who-cares-about-the-electorate, diplomatic gaffe-making, bureaucratic stasis… Yes, it's business as usual in the corridors of power in Nagatachō. Even the excitement of the election in 2001 of youthful Prime Minister Junichiro Koizumi was short lived. As one wry Western analyst put it: Where he stands depends on who his talking to. Fortunately, your average Tokyoite is as apolitical as a west coast surf-teen. The Japanese *Diet* (parliament) is made up of two houses as per the Westminster system. The emperor is largely a ceremonial figurehead yet still commands a great deal of respect. Tokyo itself is divided into 23 *ku* or wards.

ECONOMY

The financiers of Chiyoda-ku are sadly out of their humour. Tokyo businessmen look back to the halcyon economic boom days of the 1970s and early 80s, with a barely concealed wistfulness bordering on melancholia. The word on everyone's lips at present is *fukeiki* – the depressed economy. Japan is currently in the grips of its worst recession since the war and despite occasional blips of feeble optimism on the economic sonar, the overall mood is one of resigned despair.

The culprit is widely recognised as the shock of the late 1980s bursting of the 'bubble economy', but

> ### Figure Out Tokyo
> **¥20,200,000** the record price for an oceanic *bonito* sold at Tsukiji.
> **1583** the number of Tokyo pachinko parlours
> **¥11,800,000** the cost of a square metre of prime Ginza real estate
> **20-1** the ratio of Tokyoites to vending machines
> **780,000** the number of commuters who pass through Shinjuku station daily

John McInnes

the Asia-wide financial collapse, ineffectual government response, and tough competition from the USA are all key factors. Tellingly, the CEO of McDonald's Japan recently predicted the slump would last another ten years, halved the price of Big Macs (making them half Macs?) and sales increased ten-fold.

Unemployment has risen and the concept of 'a job for life' is no longer taken for granted by the younger generation. Part-time employment is on the rise. The government has recently taken to distributing shopping vouchers to the elderly and families to help boost the economy but with little success. Occasionally single thirty- or forty-somethings who live with their parents are blamed for the sluggish economy – they should be consuming more (homewares, cars etc) instead of 'sponging', say the experts.

ARTS

Tokyo is the cultural centre of Japan. The city itself is a favourite with Western artists, whether they be writers, performers or visual artists. Both traditional and contemporary culture can be experienced in the city's first class cultural centres or on the street. There is probably too much to choose from, in fact. Here's an overview of some of Tokyo's cultural highlights.

Visual Art

Tokyo's contemporary art scene is thriving. Its galleries possess a lack of pretension that is startlingly refreshing – its easy to walk into a show and start a conversation with the artists themselves. A far cry from the anti-septic, snoot-filled boxes of Manhattan or London. Perhaps this is because many of the city's painters, potters, photographers and dancers live a schiz-ophrenic creative life, forced to work day jobs to afford the hefty gallery costs in this space-starved metropolis. Progressive spaces like Art Space Ginza (installations and video), the Parco Gallery (photography), and the Pink Cow (various) in Harajuku give space to exciting work, much by the talented young artists of the city's prestigious art colleges, most notably Tama University of Fine Arts and Musashino College of Art.

The bigger museums tend to go for big names. Rodin, Renoir, Da Vinci, Degas. Their paintings are always popping into Tokyo, indeed some live there permanently. The superstars of Western art are most oft-found at the Museum of Western Art (Ueno) and the National Museum of Modern Art in Takebashi. However, don't surprised if they pop up, along with their Japanese counterparts in the department store galleries dotted around town. The commercial giants have always enjoyed flaunt-ing their 'cultural side'. The largest concentration of galleries, roughly 400, are in Ginza, most concen-trated around Ginza.

Frank Carter

Kabuki performers backstage

Performance Arts

Kabuki, nō, and *bunraku* puppet theatre are well represented throughout the city. Catching a performance of kabuki at Kabuki-za in Ginza is a must. The staging and spectacle is unforgettable. Japanese *taiko* drumming is where music meets martial art. If Niigata's Kodō happen to be in town, taking a break from their perennial world tours, you must catch a performance.

Tokyo is a mecca for Japan's enigmatic, challenging modern dance form, *butō*. Its bizarre movements, weird lighting, and long periods of inaction are not everyone's cup of green tea. Performances may take place in odd, 'non-theatrical' venues. Check with the TIC, or *Tokyo Journal*. Try to see Dairakudakan (the Great Camel Battleship), Sankaijuku, or most powerful of all, Taihen, whose members are all severely physically handicapped.

Film

Tokyo has a thriving film industry. Motion pictures were first imported from the West in 1896. The 1950s are generally considered the golden age of Japanese cinema. The most famous director of that era, Kurosawa Akira led Japanese cinema onto the main stage when his *Rashōmon* (1950) took top prize at the Venice Film Festival. Oshima Nagisa's *Ai No Corrida* (In The Realm of the Senses), a controversial tale of an obsessive love, was banned in many countries when it was released in 1976. Itami Jūzō's *Tampopo* (1985) is a wonderful comedy about sex and food – 'Zen and the art of noodle making', as one critic described it. More recently, the films of Kitano Takeshi have been warmly received around the world: check out *Hana-Bi* (1997).

Literature

If you're not familiar with Japanese literature, a good place to start is with Lady Murasaki Shikibu's *The Tale of Genji*, a collection of classic tales of early Japanese court life. Murakami Ryū's *Almost Transparent Blue* is set in the 1970s on the outskirts of Tokyo. It was a blockbuster in its day as it frankly explored a life of promiscuous sex and drug use on the fringes of Tokyo society. Murakami Haruki is the bestselling author of contemporary nonconformist works such as *A Wild Sheep Chase* and *The Wind-up Bird Chronicle*.

Music

Japan has the second-largest domestic record market in the world and consequently Tokyo is very much a part of the international live-music circuit. Most of the top performers from every genre of contemporary and classical music do shows here. Some of Tokyo's better known exports include composer Sakamoto Ryūichi, former member of *The Yellow Magic Orchestra,* and *Cornelius,* celebrated for his post-modern pop.

An overwhelming feature of the local music scene is the *aidoru* or 'idol singer'. Usually erring well on the side of untalented, the popularity of the aidoru is generated through media appearances and a carefully manufactured image. In complete contrast to commercial 'pops' is the prevalence of the local punk scene. Underground gigs, or 'live house', occur almost every night of the week in basement bars, mostly on the west side of Tokyo.

SOCIETY & CULTURE

The life of the average Japanese citizen is hidebound by a massive societal network of obligation and counter-obligation to family, colleagues, seniors, juniors, the guy next door, ancestors who shuffled off their mortal coil several generations ago – the list is endless. Those individuals who just can't stand it flee – to Tokyo. The anonymity of the megalopolis is a magnet for misfits, rebels, artists, musos, nerds and all the famous 'nails that stand out' (and duly get bashed down) in mainstream Japanese society. Thus it is, in many senses, the 'free-est' of Japanese cities. People scarcely know their neighbours, or care to. Everyone gets on with their own private lives.

Yet there's the downside. With the disintegration of the family, the continuing economic woes and the rise of a disaffected, alienated youth, Japan in general, and Tokyo in particular, is no longer the haven of safe, orderly behaviour it once was. Violent crime is rising, as is drug abuse. The generation gap between parent – schooled in convention, self-abnegation, and loyalty to 'the lifetime employer' – and the isolated, tattooed, pierced, part-time-employee child, has never been greater. It's a time of social upheaval in Japan, and all the more interesting for that.

All photographs by John Ashburne

Etiquette

Given Tokyo's distinctly different place in Japanese society it's pretty hard to offend. Anyway, Japanese people are highly forgiving of foreign visitors' minor social gaffes or indiscretions. Indeed, the older generation is trying to inculcate 'correct' social behaviour in its own offspring *who should know better!*

Foreigners or *gaijin* get cut a lot of slack. However there are a few rules of etiquette that must always be followed. When entering a house or *tatami* (straw mat) room, always take off your shoes. This rule can also apply to restaurants. If in doubt, do what everyone else does. It's bad form to blow your nose in public. The done thing is a stoic and noisy sniffle maintained until in private. Eating (except for ice cream) while walking down the street is also out. For those in Tokyo on business, *meishi* (business cards) carry a lot of weight in society and are ritually exchanged on first meetings. It's good form to accept a card with both hands and examine it before putting it away. Don't write on a card that someone has given you, at least not in their presence.

highlights

Tokyo offers a glimpse into both the future – as the modern metropolis par excellence – and Japan's fascinating past. A well-rounded visit should discover both. For high tech, visit Akihabara to discover the electronic whizzery that make's the city tick or explore some of the showrooms of Ginza. A visit to funky Harajuku and Omote-sandō should satisfy curiosity about hip Tokyo. Ueno-kōen park is also a good way to experience the human side of the city.

There are a plethora of museums to visit. The Edo-Tokyo Museum and the Tokyo National Museum, listed in this chapter, are the most significant ones and are great places to learn more about the history of Tokyo. Taking a river cruise along the Sumida-gawa is another excellent way of taking in both old and new sights. And of course no visit to Tokyo, or indeed Japan, would be complete without a visit to a significant shrine or temple such as Meiji-jingū shrine or Sensō-ji temple. Traditional culture still thrives in this metropolis and is quite accessible to visitors. Kabuki theatre and sumō are the most popular and accessible. For the Japanese take on modern culture, the John Lennon Museum is a must.

Tokyo Lowlights
- Early morning station platform vomit
- Smoke-filled restaurants
- Cover charges for Roppongi bars
- Sardine tin rush-hour hell
- Snotty Aoyama boutique assistants

Stopping Over?

One Day Get up with the larks to explore Tsukiji market. Wander through the external market, then stroll to Ginza for a leisurely lunch. Spend the afternoon exploring its galleries and gigantic department stores. Finish the day with *yakitori* (fried chicken) and a refreshing lager beneath the tracks in Yūrakuchō.

John Ashburne

Shinjuku station during peak hour

Two Days Spend the morning getting cultured in the Tokyo National Museum and people-watching in Ueno-kōen park. Then cruise the Yamanote line to Kanda for *soba* (buckwheat noodles) in one of its three celebrated restaurants. Spend the afternoon exploring the electronics capital, Akihabara, before heading out for a dinner and a night on the Roppongi tiles.

Three Days Explore Asakusa's Sensō-ji temple, then break for lunch in one of its famous local restaurants, before wandering through the streets of Shitamachi. Then skip around the Yamanote line to Harajuku and the cafes and boutiques of Omote-sandō. Round off the day with a slap-up meal at one of the city's finest restaurants.

AKIHABARA (13)

Deedle-deedle dum-dum, deedle-deedle-DEE! Buy-this-cheap-computer-chip and manga-comic-accessorEEE! The incessant tape-recorded sales jingles, delivered with high-pitched, full-volume, pseudo-prepubescent-female-intensity smack you in the face the minute you leave the sanctuary of Akihabara station.

INFORMATION

- Hibiya line to Akihabara, Electric Town exit
- Yamanote line to Akihabara, Electric Town exit
- Jangara Rāmen Honten, Kanda Yabu Soba & Matsuya (p. 74)

Martin Moos

Welcome to *Denki-gai*, Electric Town, and Japanese techno-sales gone haywire. It's something akin to the maddest Asian market you've ever been in, but instead of selling mangosteens they're hawking motherboards and the sellers are not only pushy, they're prerecorded.

Akihabara is where science fiction author, William Gibson, might shop for groceries. All virtual life is here. Too much of it. Once the dominant centre for discounted cameras, then videos, then comput-ers, today's Akihabara peddles porno-manga, the Gameboy vision of the future and yes, still, discounted electronics. There's even a valve-radio nerd's mecca in there somewhere. Enjoy. And escape… clutching purchases. Deedle-deedle dum-dum, deedle-deedle-DEE!

Even used computers are for sale in Electric Town.

John Ashburne

DON'T MISS

- plastic dolls making the latest virtual characters 'real' • bargain bins full of real electronic bargains • legions of Japan's *otaku* or cyber-nerds • Tokyo's finest noodle restaurants

EBISU GARDEN PLACE (7, D5)

It's not a garden, but it is a place and a fascinating one at that. You could wander around in here for days. This mega-complex of shops and restaurants, atop the JR Ebisu station, is a must-see. Topped with a 39-floor tower surrounded by an open mall, it's perfect for lazy summer evenings.

Ebisu Garden Place also features the headquarters of Sapporo Breweries and their **Beer Museum Yebisu**. There are lots of interesting exhibits here, the best of which is the 'Tasting Lounge', where you can sample Sapporo's various brews in a pleasant space decorated with, er, rare European beer steins.

Outdoor cafes scattered around the complex serve light meals as well as cappuccino and alcoholic drinks. The restaurants on the 38th and 39th floors of **Ebisu Garden Place Tower** offer excellent views of Tokyo, and on the ground floor the magnificent Taillevent-Robuchon restaurant out-Frenches the gallic brethren themselves with top-notch cuisine.

Ebisu Garden Place is also home to the world-class **Tokyo Metropolitan Museum of Photography**. It is the city's largest, most progressive photographic exhibition space. Its archival collection alone is as good as anything you'll find in London or New York, and the visiting shows are a good mix of the classic and the avant-garde. The wing devoted to computer-generated graphics is highly regarded.

INFORMATION

- Shibuya-ku, Ebisu 4-20
- ☎ 5423 7111; 5423 7255 Beer Museum Yebisu; 3280 0099 Metropolitan Museum of Photography
- Yamanote line to Ebisu, east exit
- Tues-Sun 10am-6pm
- free; Metropolitan Museum of Photography ¥500
- good
- many restaurants & bars on site

YEBISU BEER

DON'T MISS • the photo museum's mind-blowing computer graphics • freshly brewed Sapporo Yebisu beer • Taillevent-Robuchon's perfect imitation of a Louis XV French chateau (p. 73)

EDO-TOKYO MUSEUM (3, F10)

This splendid, huge modern museum is plonked rather obtrusively next to the sumō stables and workshops of blue-collar Ryōgoku. That's quite appropriate really, as the museum's task is to recreate Tokyo's rise from the humble riverside origins of Edo (the Eastern capital) to today's super futuristic metropolis.

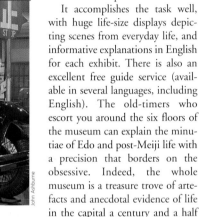

INFORMATION

- ✉ Sumida-ku, Yokoami 1-4-1
- ☎ 3272 8600
- 🚇 Toei Ōedo line to Ryōgoku, exit 4a
- 🕐 Tues-Sun 10am-6pm
- 💲 ¥600
- ℹ excellent multilingual & Braille guides
- e www.edo-tokyo-museum.or.jp/ museum-e/guide.htm
- ♿ excellent
- ✗ cafe & restaurant

It accomplishes the task well, with huge life-size displays depicting scenes from everyday life, and informative explanations in English for each exhibit. There is also an excellent free guide service (available in several languages, including English). The old-timers who escort you around the six floors of the museum can explain the minutiae of Edo and post-Meiji life with a precision that borders on the obsessive. Indeed, the whole museum is a treasure trove of artefacts and anecdotal evidence of life in the capital a century and a half ago. Feel free to wander about on your own as well and have a hands-on experience of Tokyo's past.

The unusual architecture of the Edo-Tokyo Museum

DON'T MISS • life-size replica of the Chōju Shimbun Newspaper Offices • 'Tokyo at War' display • real Edo-era Nihonbashi bridge • Model A Ford 4-door sedan taxi

GINZA   (12, G4)

Ginza is famed for its glitzy upmarket boutiques and karaoke bars run by expensive glitzy mama-sans. Getting the picture? Ginza likes to show off its status. It is also renowned for its excellent, upmarket department stores – try Wakō, Mitsukoshi and Matsuya for starters – and some of the most valuable real estate on the planet.

INFORMATION

- 🚇 Ginza, Hibiya & Marunouchi lines to Ginza
- ℹ️ TIC handout
- ✕ Maxim's de Paris & Chichibu Nishiki (p. 78)

But that's just one aspect of Ginza. It also has top-notch traditional *izakaya* and spiffy Western restaurants, good cinemas and interesting architecture. In the 1870s, Ginza was one of the first Tokyo suburbs to modernise, featuring novel Western innovations such as brick buildings, sidewalks and, that startling emblem of modernity, the gas lamp.

If innovation and creativity (coupled with an eye on the profit margins) are emblematic of Ginza, then nowhere is this more evident than in its art galleries. Ginza is chock-full of 'em, each hoping to promote the Japanese art world's Next Big Thing. Most are free to enter and gallery hopping makes a lovely break between those arduous bouts of parting with heaps of cash everywhere else you go.

But for all the glitz of Ginza, notice the chanting Buddhist monk amid the commercial chaos. Such cameos make it all worth while.

No it's not a Beatles' album cover – it's a busy intersection in Ginza.

DON'T MISS
- Wakō department store's window displays • Ginza's neon forest by night • shopping, eating, browsing in the ever-entertaining Sony Building

HARAJUKU & OMOTE-SANDŌ   (6)

Harajuku is plastic, pastel (for this week at least), youth-oriented fashion. Omote-sandō is cooler-than-a-Parisian-champagne-bucket trendy. Somehow they rub shoulders without even a murmur of conflict.

The 'highlights' of this strip south of Yoyogi-kōen park are its inhabitants, every last one out to make a fashion statement. Just wander around soaking it all up. Harajuku youth are into cute and carefree. The chic of Omote-sandō are into Chanel and cappuccino. Who cares if no-one is *really* from Tokyo at all – they're from Gunma, Niigata, or Yamanashi – but they're *here*.

Then there's the *Cos-play-zoku*. Costume Play Gang are mainly teenage girls from the dormitory towns and cities around Tokyo, who assemble at Harajuku's Jingū-bashi (the bridge linking Meiji-jingū shrine with Omote-sandō) each weekend, bedecked in Gothic make-up – a mixture of S&M, queen arch-vamp, black taffeta, blue lipstick and cartoon-nurse exaggeration. They are united in their fondness for Japanese *'visu-al-kei'* (visual-type) bands, such as L'Arc En Ciel and Zard, and a sense of pride in their alienation. Many of the girls are *'ijime-ko'*, kids bullied in school, who find release and expression in their temporary weekend identities.

The result is Tokyo's most fun circus, as each weekend hordes of excited photographers, bewildered tourists and plain voyeurs gather to catch the show. The girls revel and primp and pose for the cameras till dusk, when they hop back on the trains for the slow return to 'normal' life in the faceless housing blocks of Chiba and Kawasaki.

INFORMATION

- 🚇 Chiyoda line to Meiji-jingūmae, exit 2
- 🚉 Yamanote line to Harajuku, Omote-sandō exit
- ✕ Home, Fujimama's & L'Amphore (p. 76)

John Ashburne

DON'T MISS
- teen-fashion madness everywhere • Takeshita-dōri's boutiques
- cafe-lined boulevard Omote-sandō • young buskers on Jingū-bashi

JOHN LENNON MUSEUM   (1, B3)

The small crowd of reverential visitors is ushered into a tiny auditorium, the lights dim, the curtains part and the strains of John Lennon's ballad 'Love' fill the room. A projector clatters into life and a familiar face appears on the screen, but it's not that of Liverpool's most beloved son. Rather, it's the owner of the Lennon copyright and now merchandiser of the Lennon myth, Yoko Ono. Welcome to the John Lennon Museum, Incorporated.

Set on the 4th and 5th floors of the brand-spanking new, architecturally spectacular Saitama Super Arena, from the moment you cough up the hefty entrance fee to the moment you spill out into the ubiquitous souvenir shop (Roll up! Get your 'War is Over' toothbrush holder here!) there's a pervading sense that we're being spoon-fed a sanitised version of Lennon history.

Divided into nine zones ranging from childhood history, through The Beatles, Imagine, The Lost Weekend and, er, House Husband, the major landmarks of John's life – carefully edited for minimum offence – are delineated. No 'Beatles Bigger than Jesus'. No Nazi salute on the steps of Liverpool Town Hall to a crowd of 200,000. John Lennon's first wife, Cynthia Powell, has been Yoko-ed out of the picture altogether.

Yet for the tourist, the Beatle fan and the casual student of 20th century pop history it is somehow still enthralling, unmissable. A suitable epitaph for the man who, when once asked what he'd do when Beatlemania subsided, answered 'Count the money'.

INFORMATION

- ✉ Saitama-ken, Kami-Ochiai 2-27, Saitama Super Arena
- ☎ 048 601 0009
- 🚃 Keihin Tōhoku, Utsunomiya & Takasaki train lines to Shin-Toshin, main exit (40 mins from Tokyo)
- ⌚ Tues-Mon 11am-6pm
- 💲 ¥1500/1000
- ⓘ English captions
- e ww.taisei.co.jp/museum
- ♿ excellent
- ✗ restaurant

John Ashburne

John Ashburne

DON'T MISS
• Lennon's psychedelic schoolboy newspaper • Yoko Ono at every twist and turn • the lacquered Yamaha Folk Guitar • rude lyrics on the final display – in English only

KABUKI-ZA   (12, G5)

Of all Japan's traditional performing arts, *kabuki* is the most accessible to a non-Japanese audience. Kabuki began in the early 17th century and its first exponent was a maiden of Izumo Taisha shrine who led a troupe of women dancers to raise funds for the shrine. It caught on and was soon being performed with prostitutes in the lead roles. With performances

John Ashburne

INFORMATION

✉ Chūō-ku, Ginza
   4-12-15
☎ 3541 3131
⊕ Hibiya & Toei
   Asakusa lines to
   Higashi-Ginza, exit 3
⊙ 11am-3.50pm, 4.30-
   9.30pm
⑨ ¥2400-14,000
ⓘ English earphone
   guide ¥600/¥1000
   deposit
♿ good
✗ 6 restaurants

plumbing even greater depths of lewdness, women were banned from kabuki. They were promptly replaced with attractive young men of no less availability. The exasperated authorities issued another decree, this time commanding that kabuki roles be performed by older men.

Without doubt *the* place to see a kabuki performance is at this theatre in Ginza. Earphone sets providing excellent 'comments and explanations' in English are available. Kabuki performances are long but inevitably spectacular.

John Ashburne

A kabuki model from the Edo-Tokyo Museum

DON'T MISS
• a 'Super-Kabuki' show by rebel, pop-glam king, Ennosuke
• the architecturally significant theatre building • spectacular costumes and make-up

MEIJI-JINGŪ SHRINE (3, J2)

This is without a doubt Tokyo's, if not Japan's, most splendid Shintō shrine. Completed in 1920, Meiji-jingū was constructed in honour of Emperor Meiji and Empress Shōken. Unfortunately, it was obliterated less than 30 years later, like much of Tokyo, by WWII incendiary bombing.

Up it sprang again, next door to Yoyogi-kōen park, in 1958. It might be a reconstruction, but unlike so many others, it was rebuilt with all the features of a Shintō shrine preserved: the main building with Japanese cypress, the huge *torii* shrine gate with cypress from Ali Shan in Taiwan.

Frederic A Silva

In the grounds of the shrine (on the left, before the second *torii* gate) is **Meiji-jingū-gyoen**, the oft-deserted park, formerly an imperial garden. It has some very peaceful walks and is almost deserted on weekdays.

Meiji-jingū is also a popular spot for weddings and the subsequent photo sessions, on weekends and public holidays. On New Year's Eve it is the focus, for young and old alike, of Shintō celebrations in the city.

Chris Mellor

The entrance gate to Meiji-jingu shrine

DON'T MISS

- *Cos-play-zoku* posing on Jingū-bashi bridge • blooming irises in June • elaborate displays of traditional archery in Jan, Oct & Nov

SENSŌ-JI TEMPLE   (11, A4)

Sensō-ji temple could sit there lording it over Asakusa like a grand old dame. But actually it's more like a crusty old uncle, a little stern, not a little worldly-wise and friendly in a distant manner. The personification is not inappropriate. Sensō-ji may attract millions of tourists annually, but it is still very much a living, working temple for the people of vibrant, working-class Asakusa.

INFORMATION

- ✉ Taitō-ku, Asakusa 2-3-1
- ☎ 3842 0181
- Ⓔ Toei Asakusa & Ginza lines to Asakusa, exits 2 & 6
- ◷ 6am-5pm
- Ⓢ free
- ⓘ helpful booth opposite Kaminari-mon gate
- ♿ good
- ✗ Tonkyū, Raishūken & Owariya (p. 75)

David Ryan

Indeed, Sensō-ji's very origins are intertwined with the history of the local people. Legend has it that a golden image of Kannon, the Goddess of Compassion, was miraculously fished out of the nearby Sumida-gawa river by two fishermen in 628 AD. In time, a temple was built to house the image, which has remained on the spot ever since, giving it its alternative name, Asakusa Kannon-dō.

A traditional pagoda overlooks the courtyard of the Sensō-ji temple.

Living History

Every day, somewhere in this high-tech, ultra-modern metropolis, an event takes place that probably harks back to centuries before Christ. The **matsuri**, or festival, is an integral part of Japanese culture. Often they date back to the primitive early days of communal rice-cultivation, when townships would gather to propitiate the gods and consume vast amounts of fermented 'rice wine'. Do we detect a historical continuum? Listen for the sound of *taiko* (drums) and *yokobue* (flutes), and look for crowds in traditional *happi* half-coats carrying *mikoshi* (portable shrines). Or call the TIC for info. *Matsuri* are a daily highlight.

Approaching Sensō-ji from Asakusa subway station, enter through **Kaminari-mon** (Thunder Gate) between the scowling protective deities: Fūjin, the god of wind, on the right; and Raijin, the god of thunder, on the left.

Straight on through the gate is **Nakamise-dōri**, a shopping street set within the actual temple precinct. Everything from tourist trinkets to genuine Edo-style crafts is sold here. There's even a shop selling wigs to be worn with a kimono. Be sure to try the *sembei* (savoury rice crackers) that a few shops specialise in – you'll have to queue, though, as they are very popular with Japanese tourists as well.

Nakamise-dōri leads to the main temple compound, but it is hard to say if the Kannon image really is inside, as you cannot see it. Not that this stops a steady stream of worshippers making their way up the stairs to the temple, where they cast coins, clap ceremoniously and bow in a gesture of respect.

In front of the temple is a large incense cauldron where people go to rub smoke against their bodies to ensure good health. If any part of your body (as far as modesty permits) is giving you trouble, you should give it particular attention when applying the smoke.

DON'T MISS
• hunting for souvenirs in Nakamise-dōri • pigeons swimming in the 'holy water' • people-watching in the backstreets around the temple

SUMIDA-GAWA RIVER CRUISE   (11, C5)

OK, it's not the Seine, yet the 40-minute boat ride from Asakusa down to Ōdaiba brings you closer to Tokyo's river-borne heritage than any amount of *terra firma* temple-crawling ever could. Locked in by concrete and plexiglass, it's easy to forget that Tokyo's vibrant river systems are the arteries through which its commerce has traditionally flowed from the Edo period to today.

INFORMATION

✉ Taitō-ku, Asakusa
    Azumabashi-mae
Ⓣ Toei Asakusa &
    Ginza lines to
    Asakusa, exits 4 & 5
🕑 9.30am-6pm (once
    or twice an hour)
⑤ ¥660-1100
ⓘ English commentary
    & pamphlet
♿ good

Martin Moos

Down at water level you see the timber- and landfill-hauling giant barges, the sports fishermen and the *yakata-bune* – floating restaurants, where customers traditionally eat *ayu*, sweet fish washed down with sake, atop tatami mats. Alas, these are a dying breed.

As you head downstream from the Azuma-bashi pier in Asakusa, you'll pass under 12 bridges, each painted a different colour, en route for Hinode pier, then the 'entertainment island' Ōdaiba. Either hop off to take in the beautiful gardens at **Hama Rikyū** (p. 42) or stay on till Aomi and the delights of the **Museum of Maritime Science** (p. 45) or **Venus Fort** (p. 39). The last boat that'll get you to Hama Rikyū leaves Asakusa at 3.25pm.

A passenger ferry on the Sumida-gawa river

DON'T MISS
- great view of Philippe Starck's Asakusa landmark 'the golden turd'
- cityscape views from water level • fishermen in traditional garb heading for Tsukiji

SUMŌ WRESTLING (3, F10)

If you're in town during January, May or September, you'd be crazy not to go see the *sumō*. As a spectacle, it is stunning. As sport, it is very exciting. As a living history lesson, it's a chance to see how Shintō impacted ordinary peoples lives. Sumō's whole visual vocabulary is infused with Shintōist motifs and ideas. Study it just a little and the fat-guy-in-diapers image soon disappears. This is an ancient, disciplined, tough sport. But best of all, it's seriously fun. The rules are simple: the victor causes any part of his opponent's body other than his feet to touch the ground inside the ring (*dōyo*), or pushes him outside the ring. Sumō wrestlers look like enormous flabby infants but that flab conceals a lot of muscle.

The action during the contests, or *basho*, takes place at the **Kokugikan Sumō Hall**. The best seats are bought up by those with the right connections. Non-reserved seats at the back sell for ¥1500, and if you don't mind standing, you can get in for around ¥500. Simply turn up on the day but get there early as keen punters start queuing the night before. Only one ticket is sold per person to foil scalpers.

When a tournament isn't in session, you can enjoy the neighbouring **Sumō Museum** with its displays of humungous wrestler hand-prints, and the referees' ceremonial clothing.

Even more fun is a visit to a **sumō-beya** (wrestling stable), so that you can witness *rikishi* – literally, 'the power men' – close-up. The most famous of all is **Kokonoe Beya**, run by the legendary wrestler-turned-big-boss, Chiyonofuji the Wolf, and you are invited to 'just turn up'.

Martin Moos

Richard I'Anson

DON'T MISS • young *rikishi* lounging around in casual kimono • partisan crowds cheering on their favourite man • salt-throwing & bow-twirling rituals • marvellous sumō-related paraphernalia & souvenirs

TOKYO NATIONAL MUSEUM (10, A4)

This is a magnificent, unmissable museum and by far the best rainy-day option in the megalopolis. The Tokyo Kokuritsu Hakubutsukan, to give it its Sunday name, is an awe-inspiring collection of 89,000 supreme examples of Japanese and Asian art, variously donated and plundered from across the region.

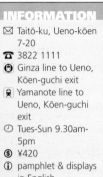

The museum actually comprises three separate museums, taking up a vast area in the eastern section of Ueno-kōen park: The **Honkan**, or main building, displays swords, ceramics, masks, metalwork and sculpture on its first floor, woodblock prints, gorgeous lacquerware and *byōbu* screens on the second. Most impressive of all is its **Gallery of Hōryūji Treasures**, featuring 300 priceless antiquities that once belonged to Hōryūji temple in Nara. As some of the exhibits are more than a thousand years old, this building remains closed during humid or wet weather.

The **Tōyōkan** is the repository for non-Japanese Asian art and antiquities. The majority is from China and Korea, with some pieces dating back to the bronze era. Its displays are changed regularly.

The third piece in this fascinating cultural and artistic jigsaw is the **Hyōkeikan**, displaying both visiting exhibits and a superb collection of ancient Japanese art and primitive sculpture dating back to the Jōmon period, before 7000BC. Try to visit when you're not in a rush, get there early and avoid national holidays and weekends.

Top: Ukiyo-e print by Toshusai Sharaku
Above: Dancing terracotta tomb figurine, Saitama, 6th century

Tokyo National Museum

DON'T MISS
- Hyōkeikan's ancient, odd-shaped Haniwa sculptures • exquisite statue of Kannon (Alokitesvara, Sanskrit) in the Gallery of Hōryūji Treasures • rotating exhibitions of Japanese lacquerware

TSUKIJI SHIJO WHOLESALE & EXTERNAL MARKETS   (12, H6)

Or just plain Tsukiji to its friends. You must visit this gigantic pulsating heart at the centre of Tokyo's gastronomic system. Its sheer scale is staggering. It serves around 12 million customers each day. In any given 24 hours its fish section alone pushes an astonishing 4000 tons of seafood worth around ¥3,000,000,000.

Yet it's not just the size of Tsukiji that impresses. There's its incredible, frenetic, fish-fuelled energy. Workers yell, slice blocks of ice, haul gigantic bluefin tuna, spit, stop for a smoke, laugh, bone an eel, yell some more… Watching the rough-and-ready, hard-working market men and women of Tsukiji, you can imagine the massive creative communal energy that allowed Tokyo to rise, in less than 200 years, from riverside swamp to one of the world's greatest cities. It's positively dizzying.

Tsukiji keeps market hours so it's good to get there early. Around 5am is best, when trading begins in earnest. Wear old shoes – there's a lot of muck and water on the floor – and don't get run down by the electric carts that hurtle along the narrow aisles.

By 10am everything quietens down. That's a good time to move out into the nearby streets and the Tsukijijō-gaishijō external market, north-west of the wholesale market, where hundreds of little stalls sell pottery, cooking equipment, food supplies, baskets, cutlery and packaged foods for a fraction of the prices charged by department stores. This is great souvenir-hunting territory and opportunities for great photographs abound.

Before you leave, drop by to see the **Namiyoke-jinja shrine** where wholesalers and middlemen come to pray and give thanks for a good day's business.

INFORMATION

- ✉ Chūō-ku, Tsukiji 5-2-1
- ☎ 3542 1111
- Ⓜ Hibiya & Toei Ōedo lines to Tsukiji, exits 1 & 3
- 🕐 Mon-Sat 5am-1.30pm
- Ⓢ free
- Ⓔ www.shijou.metro .tokyo.jp
- ✕ Tsukiji Sushikō (p. 80)

John Ashburne

Oliver Strewe

DON'T MISS • 5am bluefin tuna auctions • sushi breakfasts in the shops that fringe the market • cooling spring waters of Namiyoke-jinja shrine

UENO-KŌEN PARK   (11, B3)

This is where Tokyo comes to unwind, date, have illicit encounters, spruce up its *shamisen* (banjo) technique, practise obscure and potentially life-threatening break dance sequences. OK, it houses dozens of museums, temples, shrines, a zoo, a pond and Tokyo's most architecturally adventurous police box. But its greatest attribute is that it's a park, *a park in Tokyo*. You'll see folks here who you never dreamed existed.

John McInnes

This park has several names: its Sunday name, which no-one ever uses, is Ueno Onshi Kōen; the locals dub it Ueno no Oyama; and Westerners call it Ueno Park.

Ueno Hill was the site of a last-ditch defence of the Tokugawa Shōgunate by about 2000 Tokugawa loyalists in 1868. They were duly dispatched by the imperial army and the new Meiji government decreed that Ueno Hill would become one of Tokyo's first parks. Today, Ueno-kōen is Ueno's foremost attraction. It's home to major recommended attractions such as the **Tokyo National Museum** (p. 28), **Kokuritsu Kagaku Hakubustukan** (p. 35), **Kokuritsu Seiyō Bijitsukan** (p. 35) and the **Tokyo Metropolitan Museum of Art** (p. 37).

There are two entrances to the park. The main one takes you straight into the museum and art gallery area. It's better to start at the southern entrance near Ueno station and do a little temple viewing on the way to the museums. Slightly to your right at the top of the stairs is the mother-of-all meeting places, the **Saigō Takamori statue**. This image of a samurai walking his dog proves that between hacking each other to pieces, samurai had the time for more domestic pleasures.

Bear to the far left and follow the wide tree-lined path until you reach the temple **Kiyōmizu Kannon-dō**, modelled on Kiyōmizu-dera in Kyoto. Women who wish to conceive a child leave a doll here for the *senjū* Kannon (the 1000-armed goddess of mercy) and the accumulated dolls are burnt ceremoniously on 25 September every year.

Continue along the road following the edge of the pond **Shinobazu-ike**. Through the red *torii* (gate) is **Benten-dō**, a memorial to Benten, patron

DON'T MISS
• the spookily atmospheric Gojo fox-shrine • the itinerant 'Bear Oil' vendor • crooning sketch-artists • the magical disappearing & reappearing fountain

goddess of the arts, on an island in the pond. Behind the temple you can hire a peddle boat for 30 minutes or a row boat by the hour. Make your way back to the road that follows the pond and turn left. Where the road begins to curve and leaves the pond behind there is a stair pathway to the right. Follow the path and take the second turn to the left.

This path takes you into the grounds of **Tōshō-gō jinja**. Established in 1627 (the present building dates from 1651), this is a shrine which, like its counterpart in Nikkō, was founded in memory of Tokugawa Ieyasu. Miraculously, it has survived Tokyo's many disasters, making it one of the few early Edo structures extant. Don't miss the **Five-storey (Kanei-ji) Pagoda** to your right as you take the pathway into the shrine. The pathway is fronted by stone *torii* and lined with 200 stone lanterns given as a gift by *daimyō* (feudal lords) during the Edo period.

Under the Counter

Opposite the southern entrance to the park is **Ameyoko Arcade** (p. 62). This fascinating jumble of market-style shops, game parlours and restaurants huddled together in the shadow of the overhead Yamanote line is worth a wander. The area was famous as a black-market district in the early years following WWII and is still a lively bargain shopping area. Many of the same tourist items on sale in Ginza at inflated prices sell here at more reasonable rates. Shopkeepers are also much less restrained than those in other shopping areas in Tokyo, brazenly hawking their goods with guttural cries to the passing crowds. It is one of the few areas in which some of the rough and readiness of old Shitamachi lingers.

Crowds gather in Ueno Park to view the seasonal cherry blossoms.

sights & activities

Sightseeing in Tokyo is an exhausting business, not least as the city's neighbourhoods are far apart. While most cities have a Central Business District located at the heart of it, Tokyo is more of a collection of hubs, each imbued with it's own personality. Fortunately the subway system and circular Yamanote line combine to provide a comprehensive coverage that is staggering. You're never too far from anywhere.

The **Imperial Palace** is roughly in the centre of the Yamanote loop. Adjacent hubs **Marunouchi** and **Nihonbashi** help form the 'spiritual centre' of Tokyo with the Imperial residence, financial district and historical Tokyo station. **Ginza** is the home of Japan's first department store and still *the* place for lovers of luxury. Continuing south, **Roppongi** is notorious for its congestion of nightclubs, populated by a mix of locals and foreigners. This area is best visited by night.

The area just north of Tokyo station, **Ueno** and **Asakusa**, are also known as Shitamachi (Lower City) and generally not as upmarket as are areas like Ginza, yet should be top of the list for visitors searching for the 'real' Japan. It's also home to expansive parks and some of Tokyo's oldest shrines, temples and historical museums. Another famous area in Shitamachi is **Akihabara** with its famed 'Electric Town' for total sensory overload.

At the southern part of the loop and looking out over Tokyo Bay, **Mita**, **Tamachi** and **Shimbashi** are primarily embassy and business areas but the latter is also a gateway to **Ōdaiba** – a futuristic city built on land-fill during the bubble economy years. The monorail from Shimbashi station is driverless and it takes about 40 minutes to complete the trip.

On the west side of the loop, the east side of **Shinjuku** station is a forest of skyscrapers and the area most likely to inspire 'Blade Runner' flashbacks. The architecture to the west of Shinjuku is reminiscent of Gotham City. Shinjuku is also home to **Kabukichō** the 'pink' (or red light) area of Tokyo. Most Westerners find it relatively harmless on the surface yet a lot of Tokyoites prefer to stay away.

A couple of stops south of Shinjuku, on the Yamanote loop, lies **Harajuku**, the place where young people congregate to be seen and hopefully 'discovered'. The focus of Harajuku is **Omote-sandō**, a wide boulevard that runs from the train station (adjacent to

Off the Beaten Track

When the city drives you barmy, escape to the **Nature Study Garden** (p. 42), the leafy spaces of **Meiji-jingū** shrine (p. 23), **Yoyogi-kōen** (p. 43) or the walking paths down on **Ōdaiba** (p. 51) – all perfect getaways. Or relax with a coffee in the **World Magazine Gallery** (p. 38).

Iris Garden, Meiji-jingū shrine

Judy Bellah

the Meiji-jingū shrine) through to **Aoyama**, where you'll find the ultimate in chic eateries and fashion establishments. Lined with huge trees and Parisian-style hedges and rails, it's a joy to stroll along Omote-sandō and take in its atmosphere of space and elegance.

It's possible to walk south-east from Harajuku all the way to funky entertainment district **Shibuya**, via Harajuku Yūho-do. It's not quite as grand as Omote-sandō but it is closed to traffic. Shibuya has a bit of everything: cultural centres, art galleries, extensive shopping opportunities and some of the hippest night clubs and venues in Tokyo.

Less hip but still a hot spot for shopping is **Ikebukuro**, only a couple of Yamanote stops north of Shinjuku. Ikebukuro train and subway station is the second busiest one in Tokyo (first prize goes to Shinjuku) in terms of commuters through the ticket gates. Flanked on either side by the massive, competitive department store giants Tobū and Seibu, it's possible to spend a whole day shopping, without surfacing once for fresh air and sunlight.

It's Big, it's New & it's Coming to a Sight Near You

If you're in Tokyo during May or November, be sure to get down to the **Tokyo International Exhibition Centre**, more fondly known as **Tokyo Big Sight** (3, N10; **e** www.bigsight.co.jp; Yurikamome line to Kokusai-Tenjijō Seimon) for the twice-yearly **Design Festa**. Hundreds of young undiscovered designers rent spaces in the massive West Hall to reveal their creative genius. You might not like everything you see but there's plenty to choose from.

Where can you get your hands on a one-off T-shirt or piece of jewellery? This is it. Live entertainment in the form of free bands and the ubiquitous DJs mixin' and scratchin' make for an excellent day out. Don't be fooled though – the big saw out front is a permanent fixture.

Chris Mellor (l), Michael Taylor (r)

Visiting a Shrine or Temple

Just past the *torii* (gate) is a trough of water, or *chōzuya* with long-handled ladles perched on a rack, *hishaku,* above. This is for purifying yourself before entering the sacred precincts of the **shrine**. Some forego this ritual and head directly for the main hall. If you choose to purify yourself, take a ladle, fill it with fresh water from the spigot, pour some over one hand, transfer the spoon and pour water over the other hand. Then pour a little water into a cupped hand and rinse your mouth, spitting the water onto the ground beside (not into) the trough .

Once you've purified yourself, head to the *haiden* (hall of worship), which sits in front of the *honden* (main hall) enshrining the god of the shrine *(kami).* Toss a coin into the offerings box, ring the gong by pulling on the thick rope (to summon the deity), pray, then clap your hands twice, bow and then back away from the shrine. Amulets are sold (¥100-200) at the shrine office near the worship hall. Look for signs prohibiting photography. If it's allowed, be discreet so as not to disturb worshippers.

Unless the **temple** contains a shrine, you will not have to purify yourself before entry. The place of worship in a temple is in the *hondō,* which usually contains a Buddhist altar and one or more Buddha images. Entry is usually free; otherwise admission is around ¥500. The standard practice is to toss some change into the offerings box, which sits in front of the altar, step back, place one's hands together, pray, then bow to the altar before backing away.

Most temples sell *omikuji* (fortunes written on little slips of paper; ¥100). Pay an attendant or place the money in an honour-system box. Fortunes are dispensed randomly from a special box containing sticks with different numbers written on their ends. Shake the box until one stick drops out of a hole in its top. Take this to the attendant and you will be given a fortune matching the number on the stick. This will be written in Japanese under one of four general headings: *dai-kitchi* (big luck), *kitchi* (luck), *sho-kitchi* (small luck, moderately grim) and *kyō* (bad luck).You can also purchase amulets called *omamori* at temples. These usually cost a few hundred yen and come in a variety of shapes and sizes, the most common of which is a piece of fabric bearing the temple's name enclosed in a plastic case. Some temples have omamori for specific things like traffic safety, good health and academic success. Hello Kitty omamori are currently all the rage.

Jonathan Selig

MUSEUMS

Tokyo has splendid museums, but get there early before the crowds. Discounted ticketing has yet to catch on, but try showing ID if you feel you might be eligible. Many places charge extra for visiting exhibits.

Fukagawa Edo Museum (3, H10)
It may not be quite as good as its big brother, Edo-Tokyo Museum, but this is still a fun, funky look at Tokyo as it was during its formative years. The museum itself is located in an area that has retained some of those old Edo riverside roots.
✉ Kōtō-ku, Shirakawa 1-3-28 ☎ 3630 8625
Ⓣ Toei Ōedo line to Kiyosumi-Shirakawa, exit 3 ⓘ 9.30am-4.30pm (closed 2nd & 4th Mon of the month)
Ⓢ ¥300 ⓖ good

Hara Museum of Contemporary Art (3, O5) This is an excellent, adventurous museum that showcases contemporary art by local and international avant-garde artists. As well as exhibiting the works of controversial artists such as Gilbert & George (UK) and Cindy Sherman (US), the museum sponsors excellent workshops and presentations by those artists participating in the exhibitions.
✉ Shinagawa-ku, Kita-Shinagawa 4-7-25 ☎ 3445 0651
Ⓔ www.haramuseum .or.jp Ⓡ Yamanote line to Shinagawa, west exit; then 5mins by taxi or Tan 96 Otsu bus to Gotenyama (first stop)
ⓘ Tues-Sun 11am-5pm
Ⓢ ¥700

Idemitsu Art Museum (12, F3)
Superb eclectic collection of Chinese, Japanese and Western art, courtesy of a petroleum zillionaire. There are also very worthy views of the Imperial Palace from here. New aristocracy looking down on the old one, perhaps? It's on the 9th floor of the Kokusai building, next to Teikoku Gekijō, the Imperial Theatre.
✉ Chiyoda-ku, Marunouchi 3-1-1, Teikokugeki Bldg, 9F ☎ 3272 8600
Ⓔ www.idemitsu.co.jp/ museum

Ⓣ Yūrakuchō line to Yūrakuchō, Kokusai Forum-guchi exit
ⓘ Tues-Sun 10am-5pm
Ⓢ ¥500 ⓖ good

Kite Museum (12, C5)
This unusual museum feels like a kite-maker's store cupboard with everything crammed in as much as possible. The kites are magnificent, not least the Japanese ones. There could be a lot more explanatory material for visitors, but with a bit of imagination you can picture them in flight – high above the skyscrapers.
✉ Chūō-ku,

Relaxing in the garden of the Nezu Institute of Fine Arts

Nihonbashi 1-12-10,
Taimeiken Bldg, 5F
☎ 3275 2704
🜨 Tōzai line to
Nihonbashi, exit C5
🕙 Tues-Sun 11am-5pm
⑤ ¥200 ☿ good

Kokuritsu Kagaku
Hakubutsukan (10, B4)
The National Science
Museum has been making
an effort to modernise
itself, not least with its
Science Discovery Plaza
aimed at the teenage
audience. There's some
irony in its choice of mas-
cot – a large endangered
whale.
✉ Taitō-ku,
Ueno-kōen 7-20
☎ 3822 0111
🇪 www.kahaku.go.jp
🚇 Yamanote & Keihin-
Tōhoku lines to Ueno,
Kōen-guchi exit
🕙 Tues-Sun 9am-
4.30pm
⑤ ¥420 ☿ good

Kokuritsu Seiyō
Bijitsukan (10, B4)
It may seem odd coming all
this way just to check out
Rodin sculptures and the Le
Corbusier architecture. Yet

the Museum of Western Art
is splendid and well worth
the trip, especially during
its frequent visiting
exhibits.
✉ Taitō-ku, Ueno-kōen
7-7 ☎ 3828 5131
🇪 www.nmwa.go.jp/
🚇 Yamanote & Keihin-
Tōhoku lines to Ueno,
Kōen-guchi exit
🕙 Tues-Sun 9.30am-
7pm ⑤ ¥420 ☿ good

Nezu Institute of Fine
Arts (3, K4)
This is nirvana for all
Asian art buffs, with
exquisite ceramics and
paintings from China,
Vietnam and Japan. The
slightly wild, statue-dotted
gardens also make for a
pleasant afternoon's
escape from the conges-
tion of the Tokyo streets.
It's well signposted and
only a ten minute walk
east from the station.
✉ Minato-ku, Minami-
Aoyama 6-5-1
🇪 www.nezu-muse
.or.jp/
🜨 Chiyoda line to
Omote-sando, exit A5
🕙 9.30am-4pm
⑤ ¥1000 ☿ good

Nihonshu Jōhōkan
(12, H2) Actually a brilliant
museum showcase for
sake, sponsored by the
sake-makers' union. The
first floor features an excellent sake shop, with tastings of the very finest
hooch at ¥550 a pop. In
the 4th floor gallery, the
sake tastings are free until
5.30pm. This is the best
place in town to buy up on
your sake souvenirs.
✉ Minato-ku, Nishi-
Shimbashi 1-1-21,
Nihon Shuzo Kaikan, 1F
& 4F
☎ 3519 2091
🜨 Ginza line to
Toranomon, exit 9
🕙 10am-6.30pm
⑤ free ☿ good

Shitamachi History
Museum (10, D3)
Lots of fun here for the
historically imaginative,
poking around inside a
Shitamachi tenement
house (don't forget to
take off your shoes), or
pondering whether you
would rather have been a
copper-boiler, a sweet-
shop-owner or a merchant
in a previous Japanese
life.
✉ Taitō-ku, Ueno-kōen
2-1 ☎ 3823 7451
🚇 Yamanote & Keihin-
Tōhoku lines to Ueno,
Shinobazu-guchi exit
🕙 Tues-Sun 9.30am-
4.30pm ⑤ ¥300
☿ good

Taikokan Drum
Museum (11, C1)
Splendidly interactive exhibition space. Bash away on
any item you fancy as long
as it's not marked with a
red dot. The staff seem
used to gaijin Keith Moon
wannabes. It's on the
second floor of the

It's a Long Way to the MoT

The **Metropolitan Museum of Contemporary Art Tokyo** (Kōtō-ku, Miyoshi 4-1-1, Metropolitan Kiba Park; ☎ 5245 4111; 🇪 www. tef.or.jp/mot/eng /lobby/info-e.html) is a must for architecture buffs as well as art fans. Constructed from wood, stone, metal and glass, it manages to create an oasis of pure light and water. The museum, also known as **MoT**, hous-es a permanent collection of significant modern Japanese art. Each work has its own postcard with photo, title and artist biography written in Japanese on one side and English on the other. The special exhibitions are significant and exhausting. Take the Tōzai line to Kiba station and from there it's a mere 15 minutes walk.

Tokyo Metropolitan Museum of Art

Miyamoto festival goods store on Kokusai-dōri, opposite the koban (police box).

✉ **Taitō-ku, Nishi-Asakusa 2-1-1, Nishi-Asakusaten Bldg, 4F**
☎ **3842 5622** 🚇 **Ginza line to Tawaramachi, exit 3** 🕐 **Wed-Sun 10am-5pm** 💲 **¥300**

Tepco Electric Energy Museum (5, B3)

Suprisingly, this is one of Tokyo's better science museums, offering seven floors of dynamic exhibitions on every conceivable aspect of electricity and its production. There are innumerable displays that are hands-on and an excellent, free English handout that explains everything.

✉ **Shibuya-ku, Jinnan 1-12-8** ☎ **3477 1191** 🚆 **Yamanote line to Shibuya, Hachikō-guchi exit** 🕐 **Thurs-Tues 10am-6pm** 💲 **free** ♿ **good**

Kokuritsu Kindai Bijitsukan (12, E5)

Scheduled to reopen after renovation in late 2001, the National Museum of Modern Art has a magnificent collection of Japanese art from the Meiji period onwards. The nearby Crafts Gallery houses ceramics, lacquerware and dolls.

✉ **Chūō-ku, Kitanomaru-kōen 3** ☎ **3272 8600** 📧 **www.momat.go.jp** 🚇 **Ginza line to Kyōbashi, exit 1** 🕐 **Tues-Sun 10am-5pm** 💲 **¥420** ♿ **good**

Tokyo Metropolitan Museum of Art

(10, B3) Breathtaking calligraphy and contemporary Japanese and Western paintings are housed in this museum. It is a great place to delve for hours into the creative quagmire of 20th- and 21st-century art. The great free art library is worth a browse.

✉ **Taitō-ku, Ueno-kōen 8-36** ☎ **3823 6921** 🚆 **Yamanote & Keihin-Tōhoku lines to Ueno, Kōen-guchi exit** 🕐 **9am-5pm (closed 3rd Mon of the month)** 💲 **free; special exhibits ¥900-1100** ♿ **good**

Watari Museum of Contemporary Art

(6, B4) Lots of brilliant arty-farty overload, with visiting Scandinavians choreographing vacuum-cleaner ballets, and resident Japanese embalming themselves with glue. Or that kind of thing. Plenty of cutting edge contemporary art to be found here, especially mixed-media art installations.

✉ **Shibuya-ku, Jingūmae 3-7-6** ☎ **3402 3001** 🚇 **Ginza line to Gaienmae, exit 3** 🕐 **Tues-Sun, 11am-7pm** 💲 **¥1000**

GALLERIES

Art galleries in Tokyo usually don't charge an entry fee. They tend to be smaller and less exhausting than the big museums. The largest concentration of art galleries is in Ginza, but they can also be found in the chic neighbourhoods of Shibuya, Harajuku and Aoyama.

Art Museum
Ginza (12, H4)
Spiffy little modern art gallery set on two floors. Very flash, very high-tech. Very Tokyo, then. Especially strong on video and sculptural installations. It's just down the street from the Sony building on Sotobori-dōri.
⊠ **Chūō-ku, Ginza 7-4-12, Gyōsei Bldg, B1F & 1F** ☎ **3571 2285** 🚇 **Ginza line to Shimbashi, exit 5** ⏱ **11am-5pm (days vary)** ⑤ **free** ♿ **good**

Contax Gallery (12, G4)
Contemporary Japanese photography courtesy of the camera maker. Proof that Japan's much vaunted obsession with nature is no myth – the nature and wildlife images are invariably the most impressive. Next door to the San-ai building on Chūō-dōri.
⊠ **Chūō-ku, Ginza 5-7-4, Kyūkyodō Bldg, 5F** ☎ **3572 1921** 🄴 **www .inter-g7.or.jp/g7/ gallery/contax/home-e.html** 🚇 **Hibiya, Ginza, & Marunouchi lines to Ginza, exits A1 & A2** ⏱ **Tues-Sun 10.30am-6.30pm** ⑤ **free** ♿ **good**

Nikon Salon (12, G5)
This place takes a few more chances than the Contax Gallery with occasional shows by leading overseas photographers as well as home-grown stars. More into portraiture and the 'old masters' of

photography.
⊠ **Chūō-ku, Ginza 5-11-4, Ginza Crest Bldg, 2F** ☎ **3248 3783** 🚇 **Asakusa & Hibiya lines to Higashi-Ginza, exit 2** ⏱ **Mon-Sat 10am-7pm** ⑤ **free** ♿ **good**

Parco Gallery (5, C2)
Tokyo's most progressive independent photo gallery, often exhibiting works by leading international artists such as Andreas Serrano and Joel-Peter Witkin. Recently moved from rooftop to basement.
⊠ **Shibuya-ku, Udagawachō15-1, Shibuya Parco Part 1, B1F** ☎ **3477 5873** 🚃 **Yamanote line to Shibuya, Hachikō-guchi exit** ⏱ **10am-8.30pm** ⑤ **¥500** ♿ **good**

Toyota Amlux (2, C5)
Not a gallery in the normal sense, but rather a collection of classy, expensive works of art – Toyota's flagship motor vehicles. It is five floors of blatant self-

promotion, but with neat ambient sound effects and a majestic escalator ride. It's car-nerd heaven.
⊠ **Toshima-ku, Higashi-Ikebukuro 3-3-5** ☎ **5391 5900** 🚇 **Yūrakuchō line to Higashi-Ikebukuro, exit 2** ⏱ **Tues-Sat 11am-8pm, Sun & public holidays 10am-7.30pm** ⑤ **free** ♿ **good**

World Magazine
Gallery (12, F4)
Head here in the pouring rain, or when Tokyo just gets too much, to hibernate over coffee with one of the 1200 or so magazines from around the world. It's an armchair traveller's paradise. Find out what they're wearing this year in Albania. We also suspect it's a pick-up spot.
⊠ **Chūō-ku, Ginza 3-13-10, Magazine House, 1F** ☎ **3545 7227** 🚇 **Marunouchi line to Ginza, exit C8** ⏱ **Mon-Fri 11am-7pm** ⑤ **free**

Taking it to the streets: young Harajuku artists on show.

QUIRKY TOKYO

Condomania (6, C2)
More prophylactics than you can shake a stick at – look out for glow-in-the-dark Alien Willie and condom sculptures that would look dandy on the mantlepiece back home.
✉ Shibuya-ku, Jingūmae 6-30-1
☎ 3797 6131
🚇 Yamanote line to Harajuku, Omote-sandō exit
🕐 10.30am-11pm

Criminology Museum of Meiji University (3, F7)
Meiji-Daigaku Keiji-Hakubutsukan houses a splendid collection of memorabilia celebrating centuries of criminal detection by the Japanese forces of law and order. Not really, of course. It's a prime opportunity for voyeuristic observation of the corrupt side of human nature. There's not much English, but it's still interesting.
✉ Chiyoda-ku, Kanda Surugadai 1-1, Daigaku-kaikan, 3F
☎ 3296 4431
🚇 Marunouchi line to Ochanomizu, exit B1
🚇 Chūō & Sōbu lines to Ochanomizu, south exit
🕐 Mon-Fri 10am-4.30pm, Sat 10am-12.30pm ⑤ free
♿ good

Meguro Parasite Museum (7, E2)
Aaargh! More parasites than you can shake a stick at in this museum dedicated to scary things that may have been in your lunch. The specimen that

Condomania is a popular meeting place in Harajuku, on the corner of Meiji-dōri and Omote-sandō.

John Ashburne

makes testicles swell to basketball-size proportions is, er…impressive. Brilliant gift-shop with tapeworm fridge-magnets and the like.
✉ Meguro-ku, Shita-Meguro 34-1-1
☎ 3716 1264
🚇 Yamanote line to Meguro, main exit, then any bus to Ōtori-jinjamae
🕐 Tues-Sun 10am-5pm ⑤ free ♿ good, no toilet access

Venus Fort (3, O9)
A collection of 137 boutiques and restaurants all aimed at young women, set in a building that mimics 17th-century

Rome. It comes complete with marble fountains, illuminated ceilings that constantly change colour (simulating day turning into night), and Japan's biggest lavatory (64 stalls with the promise 'you'll never need to wait in line). Perfect for the credit card toting Renaissance woman and pretty good fun for the rest of us too. There are good English pamphlets available as well.
✉ Kōtō-ku, Aomi 1, Palette Town
☎ 3599 0700
🚇 Yurikamome line to Aomi, main exit
🕐 11am-10pm, restaurants till 11pm

SIGNIFICANT BUILDINGS

Sunshine City Alpa (2, C5)

Billed as 'a city in a building' this is another opportunity to partake of that quintessential Japanese pastime: shopping. However for a small fee you can get catapulted in the world's second fastest elevator to the 60th floor observatory, and peer out across Tokyo's hazy skyline. Mt Fuji's out there somewhere. Honest. See also Sunshine International Aquarium (p. 44-5), Sunshine Planetarium (p. 45) and Toyota Amlux (p. 38).

✉ **Toshima-ku, Higashi-Ikebukuro 3-1**
☎ **3989 3331**
Ⓨ **Yūrakuchō line to Higashi-Ikebukuro, exit 2**
🕐 **10am-8.30pm**
Ⓢ **¥620 observation deck**

Tokyo Metropolitan Government Offices

(4, C1) OK, Tokyo Tochō is a Stalinesque piece of post-modern architectural and governmental arrogance, but it is, well, big. The twin towers comprising Tokyo's bureaucratic heartland are colossal, and whizzing up to the twin observation decks, 202m or so above urban Shinjuku, is a gas. Why not unwrap a rice-ball in the amphitheatre-like Citizen's Plaza below, and ponder human vanity.

✉ **Shinjuku-ku, Nishi-Shinjuku 2-8-1** ☎ **5321 1111** Ⓞ **Toei Ōedo line to Tochōmae exits A3, A4** 🕐 **Nth tower Tues-Sun 9.30am-10pm; Sth tower Wed-Mon 9.30am-5.30pm, Sat-Sun 9.30am-7pm**
Ⓢ **free** ♿ **excellent**

Tokyo International Forum (12, F4)

It's a fantastic glass ship plying the urban waters of central Tokyo. No, it's a library, home to international ATMs, free Internet access, a photo gallery and the main Tokyo Tourist Information Center (TIC). No, its a nocturnal purple and orange-hued giant space colony, into the 22nd century. Whatever it is, you'd better check it out.

✉ **Chiyoda-ku, Marunouchi 3-5-1**
☎ **3201 3331**
🅴 **www.tif.or.jp**
Ⓡ **Yamanote line to Tokyo, Marunouchi Central exit** 🕐 **8am-11pm** Ⓢ **free**
♿ **excellent**

Architecture or Anarchy?

The Tokyo cityscape is an architect's dream. Or worst nightmare. Famed buildings include the **Tochō** (Shinjuku), **Axis Building** (Roppongi), **Imperial Hotel** (Kanda), **Fuji TV Building** (Ōdaiba) and **Tokyo International Forum** (Yūrakuchō). It doesn't matter where you look, design derangement seems to be everywhere.

Tokyo International Forum

John Ashburne

Tokyo Metropolitan Government Offices

Tokyo Stock Exchange (12, B5)

Watch the Japanese economy explode to the heavens or disappear up its own stock index – all from the mundane comfort of the 2nd-floor observation deck. Not quite as mad as during the bubble economy, but still quite a show. Good tours in English, but you need to reserve in advance. With stock trading simulation games for closet rogue-traders.

✉ Chūō-ku, Kabutochō Nihonbashi 2-1
☎ 3666 0141
Ⓜ Tōzai line to Kayabachō, exit 11
🕐 Mon-Fri 9-11am, 1-4pm ⑤ free
♿ excellent

Tokyo Tower (3, K6)

Pity poor Eiffel-wannabe Tokyo Tower. It still belongs in an age when bicycle clips and fizzy pop were the latest in trendiness. Today cyber-kids barely notice it. Yet for those with a fascination for bygone girders, it offers a strange allure.

✉ Minato-ku, Shiba-kōen 4-2-8 ☎ 3433 5111 ⓔ www.tokyo tower.co.jp Ⓜ Hibiya line to Kamiyachō, exit 1 🕐 9am-8pm
⑤ observation platforms ¥ 600-820; aquarium ¥ 800; wax museum ¥ 870 ♿ good

Yasukuni-jinja (3, G5)

Perennial fly-in-the-ointment in Japan-Asia relations, it is the 'Peaceful Country Shrine'. It's also a memorial to Japan's 2.5 million or so war-dead. No wonder it invites controversy. Politics aside, it is interesting with a beautiful, contemplative inner sanctum in the style of ancient Ise shrines – a stark contrast to the right-wing activists (uyoku) shouting their rhetoric outside.

✉ Chiyoda-ku, Kudan-kita 3-1-1 ☎ 3261 8326 ⓔ www.yasukuni .or.jp Ⓜ Toei Shinjuku line to Kudanshita, exits 1 & 2
🕐 9.30am-4.30pm
⑤ free ♿ good

No it's not the latest Star Trek movie set – it's the new-look trading floor at the Tokyo Stock Exchange.

PARKS & GARDENS

Hama Rikyū Onshi-teien (12, K6)

The *shōgun* used to have this magnificent place to themselves when it was Hama Rikyū, 'the beach palace'. Now mere mortals can enjoy this wonderful garden, one of Tokyo's best. It is impossibly elegant and a must for garden addicts. Consider approaching it from Asakusa via the Sumida-gawa river cruise (see p. 26).

✉ Chūō-ku, Hamarikyū Teien 1-1
☎ 3541 0200
🚇 Toei Ōedo line to Tsukiji-shijō, exit A2
🕐 9am-4.30pm
💲 ¥300 ♿ good

Imperial Palace East Garden (12, C1)

The nearest escape from Ginza street chaos, Higashi Gyōen is a pleasant-stroll garden. Its main feature is the Edo-period watchtower, Fujimi-yagura, designed to provide the aristocracy with a handy view of Mt Fuji. Even today, the imperial household sometimes nobbles the garden for an impromptu tea-party.

✉ Chiyoda-ku, Chiyoda 1-1 ☎ 3213 1111
🚇 Tōzai line to Takebashi, exit A1
🕐 9am-4pm 💲 free
♿ good

Koishikawa Kōraku-en

(3, E6) A beautiful amalgam of Japanese and Chinese landscape design, this mid-17th-century garden is oddly left off most tourist itineraries. It's a shame, because it really is very pleasant. The helpful staff will carry wheelchairs although there are no

Private Gardens

In Tokyo they're not the rose-pruning, tomato-rearing variety. Most gardens were designed solely for looking at or strolling in, usually by ultra-wealthy aristocrats and samurai. Now they're available to the general public for a small fee.

Serene Imperial Palace East Garden was once the centre of the old castle site.

specific facilities for them.

✉ Bunkyō-ku, Kōraku-en 1-6-6
☎ 3811 3015
🚇 Toei Ōedo & Tōzai lines to Iidabashi, exit A1 🕐 9am-5pm
💲 ¥300 ♿ ok

Nature Study Garden

(3, M4) Prosaic name, but pulchritudinous garden. Unique in Tokyo, it wilfully tries to preserve Tokyo's original flora in undisciplined profusion. How un-Japanese, of it! Great city-stress-relieving walks through wild woods and swamps, making this one of Tokyo's least known and most appealing getaways.

✉ Minato-ku, Shiroganedai 5-21-5
☎ 3441 7176
🚇 Toei Asakusa line to

Takanawadai, exit A2
🕐 Tues-Sun 9am-4.30pm (summer till 5pm)
💲 ¥210 ♿ good

Rikugi-en (3, B5)

The poets' favourite, this is another garden good for strolling with landscaped views unfolding at every turn of the pathways that crisscross the grounds. Its design is said to invoke famous scenes from Chinese literature and Japanese *waka* (31-syllable) poetry.

✉ Bunkyō-ku, Hon-Komagome 6-6-13
☎ 3941 2222
🚉 Yamanote line to Komagome, south exit
🕐 9am-4.30pm
💲 ¥300 ♿ good

Blossom Rapture

Around April the whole nation excitedly waits for the first buds to appear on cherry trees. *Hanami* (cherry-blossom viewing) parties are held to celebrate the flowers during the week-long flowering season and both daytime parties and moonlit soirees are popular. There's plenty of sake, singing and dancing (beware of portable karaoke machines). At popular hanami spots the best sites are often taken by people who have camped out overnight for them. Company employees join in, often spending afternoons and evenings drinking under the blossoms. Of course, it is compulsory to join in! For more seasonal activities, see page 99.

Shinjuku-gyōen

(3, H3) Pleasant downtown park providing the perfect escape from the winter cold as it boasts a hothouse full of exotic tropical plants, including – it's rumoured – peyote! Nice, meditative carp-watching to be done here as well. Keep this park in mind when you're exhausted by all that busy Shinjuku has to offer.
✉ Shinjuku-ku, Naitōmachi 11
☎ 3550 0151
🄴 www.shinjukugoen.go.jp 🄜 Marunouchi line to Shinjuku-gyōen, exit 1 ⏲ Tues-Sun 9am-4.30pm ⑤ ¥200

Yoyogi-kōen (3, J2)

Sleepy, spacious skateboarder hang-out perched on the edge of Harajuku, and a perfect picnic spot at the heart of the city. Bring a Frisbee and a bottle of sake. At weekends enjoy the Goth-glamour shenanigans of the Costume Play Gang at nearby Jingū-bashi (p. 20). Rock, pop and punk musicians still come here to busk occasionally.
✉ Shibuya-ku, Yoyogi Kamizonochō, Jinnan 2
☎ 3469 6081
🄗 Chiyoda line to Meiji-jingūmae, exit 3
♿ excellent

Ueno-koen park is a green oasis in a desert of neon, glass and concrete.

TOKYO FOR CHILDREN

Tokyo is the perfect city to visit with children. It's colourful, stimulating and a lot of activities are fun for both generations. Be prepared for exclamations of 'kawaii' (cute) from admiring strangers, especially if you have young children. Here are a few of the places of major interest for kids. Look for 🐾 listed with individual reviews in the Places to Eat, Entertainment and Places to Stay chapters for further kid-friendly options.

Hakuhinkan Toy Park
(12, H4) Claiming to be one of the largest toy shops in the world, the Hakuhinkan Toy Park also features restaurants and theatres. Unless you're careful this is a sure-fire spot to spend your entire holiday budget (see also Shopping p. 69)
✉ Chūō-ku, Ginza 8-8-11 ☎ 3571 8008
🚉 Yamanote & Keihin-Tōhoku lines to Shimbashi, exits 1 & 3
🕐 11am-8pm
💲 free 🚻 good

National Children's Castle (5, C5)
If you bring a brood, Kodomo no Shiro is by far the most comprehensive, child-friendly complex in the city. OK, so it doesn't even look like a real castle but with its pool, indoor and rooftop play areas, and diversions for accompanying adults, who could complain? Stay next door at the Children's Castle Hotel (p. 104). Well-placed in Aoyama.
✉ Shibuya ku, Jingūmae 5-53-1
☎ 3797 5665
📧 www.kodomono-shiro.or.jp
🚉 Hanzōmon line to Shibuya, exit 5
🕐 Tues-Fri 12.30pm-5.30pm, Sat-Sun 10am-5.30pm
💲 ¥500/400 🚻 good

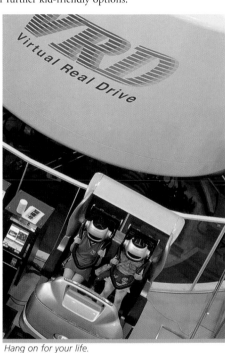

Hang on for your life.

Mega Web (3, O9)
Take a ride into the future – oh yes and bring the kids too – in the automotive Gameboy-meets-roller-coaster 3D Future World Experience. Or plug the family into the Virtual Real Drive, which has one of you piloting a speeding Toyota off a mountain precipice. Corporate self-promotion gone nuts, but serious hands-on fun. Just kidding about the precipice.
✉ Kōtō-ku, Aomi 1
☎ 3599 0808
📧 www.megaweb.gr.jp
🚉 Yurikamome to Aomi, main exit
🕐 11am-8pm; Future World 11am-10.30pm
💲 ¥200-800 per ride

Sunshine International Aquarium (2, C5)
This is probably the most

interesting place to be when the next big earthquake levels central Tokyo. Lots of nice sharks, piranhas and electric eels to commune with up on the 10th and 11th floors of this bit of Sunshine City. Not as good as the Osaka counterpart, but still fascinating.

✉ **Toshima-ku, Higashi-Ikebukuro 3-1, Sunshine Import Mart Bldg 10, 11F** ☎ **3989 3466** 🚇 **Yūrakuchō line to Higashi-Ikebukuro, exit 2** ⏱ **10am-6pm** ⑤ **¥1600/800** ♿ **good**

Sunshine Planetarium (2, C5)

We may be in down-to-earth Ikebukuro but many of us are looking at the stars… Alas, the show is narrated in Japanese but the visuals are spectacular enough to lift you out of this earthly end of Tokyo.

✉ **Toshima-ku, Higashi-Ikebukuro 3-1, Sunshine Import Mart Bldg 10F** ☎ **3989 3466**

🚇 **Yūrakuchō line to Higashi-Ikebukuro, exit 2** ⏱ **Mon-Fri noon-5.30pm, Sat-Sun 11am-6.30pm** ⑤ **¥800/500** ♿ **good**

Tokyo Disneyland

(1, C3) For some it's the last resort. For some the first. A near-perfect replica of the California original – turn left into the African Jungle, head straight on to Fantasyland and turn right to Tomorrowland. Art imitating life? You bet. A parable for modern Tokyo? Probably. Beguiling? Oh yes… Despite the crowds and queues, no-one is ever disappointed. *Ever*. Even hard-hearted cynics are won over by its colour and exuberance. It's in the sticks in Chiba, but worth the trip.

✉ **Urayasu-shi, Maihama 1-4** ☎ **047 683 3333** 🖥 **www.tokyodisney resort.co.jp** 🚇 **Keiyō line to Maihama, main exit** 🚌 **from many locations in Central Tokyo** ⏱ **9am-10.30pm**

⑤ **¥5500/4800/3700** ♿ **excellent**

Kōraku-en Amusement Park

(3, E6) Adrenalin fiends of all ages will enjoy the Spinning Coaster Maihime and the Thrill Ride. When your equilibrium has been truly scrambled, head next door to the contemplative spaces of the **Koishikawa Kōraku-en** garden (p. 42).

✉ **Bunkyō-ku, Kōraku 1-3-61** ☎ **3817 6098** 🚇 **Marunouchi line to Kōraku-en, main exit** 🚇 **Chūō line to Suidōbashi, east exit** ⏱ **Mon-Sun 10am-6pm (autumn & spring till 8pm, summer till 10pm)** ⑤ **¥ 1200/600 per ride; ¥ 3300/2600 unlimited rides**

Museum of Maritime Science **(3, O8)**

Fune no Kagaku-kan is one of Tokyo's better museums. Four floors of excellent displays, lots of hands-on exhibits, which kids will love, and a pool on the roof where, for ¥100, they can wreak havoc with

Having a whale of a time at the Museum of Maritime Science.

Martin Moos

Babysitters

Finding someone to look after the kids is not an easy task in Tokyo, not least if you're only visiting for a short period. A very popular service among the foreign community is the professional child-care service **Kids World** (☎ 0120 001527) that has native-English speakers and fun activities. Drop-in service is available at many convenient locations in central Tokyo.

Agency baby-sitters are generally either experienced grandmotherly types or part-time university students. Minimum charge is ¥1500-3000 for 2-3hrs. Some companies require you pay a hefty membership fee. Reputable agencies include: **Japan Baby-sitter Service** (☎ 3423 1251); **Kinder Network** (☎ 3486 8278); **Nihon Baby-sitter** (☎ 3822 8058) and **Poppins' Service** (☎ 3447 2100).

A handy starting point for finding private sitters is e www.tokyowithkids.com/babysitter/list/.

radio-controlled boats and submarines.
✉ Shinagawa-ku, Higashi-Yashio 3-1
☎ 5500 1111
🚇 Yurikamome line to Fune-no-kagakukan, main exit ⏰ 10am-5pm 💲 ¥1000/600
♿ good

Transportation Museum (13, C8)

This is a great place for kids and adults alike. Actually, it's trainspotter heaven. You can pretend to 'drive' a virtual JR Yamanote train around Tokyo and no-one will call you a nerd.
✉ Chiyoda-ku, Kanda Sudachō 1-25 ☎ 3251 8481 e www.kouhaku.or.jp 🚇 Marunouchi line to Awajichō, exits A3 & A5 ⏰ Tues-Sun 9.30am-5pm
💲 ¥310/150

Ueno Zoo (10, B2)

Not in the same league as its colleagues in Frankfurt or London, but visitors here are always having such a good-natured fun time, it's hard to resist the place. Displays can be cramped, but the pandas, snow leopards, gorillas and Bengal tigers are fabulous.
✉ Taitō-ku, Ueno-kōen 9-83 ☎ 3828 5171
🚇 Chiyoda line to Nezu, south exit
🚃 Yamanote & Keihin-Tōhoku line to Ueno, Kōen-guchi exit
⏰ Tues-Sun 9.30am-4.30pm 💲 ¥600/200, toddlers free ♿

A perfect afternoon excursion – the Sumida-gawa river cruise (p. 26).

KEEPING FIT

Tokyo isn't as fitness-obsessed as many big cities, though its parks and large public spaces teem with joggers and walkers (doing the odd elbows-up, vaguely militaristic Japanese version). Yoyogi-kōen, Meiji-jingū and the grounds of the Imperial Palace are especially popular. Most top-end hotels come with fitness rooms, spas and beauty centres.

Chiyoda Kuritsu Sogo Taikukan (3, G8)

Most gym-goers in Tokyo belong to private gyms. This complex is actually subsidised by the local ward for residents of that area. However visitors can use it for an additional fee. It's quite centrally located with a reasonably-sized pool and gymnasium.
✉ Chiyoda-ku, Uchi-Kanda 2-1-8
☎ 3256 8444
🚉 Yamanote line to Kanda, exit 2
🕐 noon-8.30pm
💲 ¥600

International Yoga Center (1, B3)

Popular yoga teaching center specialising in Ashtanga and Iyengar yoga. Drop in for a one-off class/session.
✉ Suginami-ku, Ogikubo 5-30-6,

Fukumura Ogikubo Bldg ☎ 090 49567996

@ welcome.to/yogatokyo
🚇 Marunouchi line to Ogikubo, south exit
🕐 Mon-Sun 6am-10am, 3pm-5pm 💲 ¥600

Mammy's Touch (6, E4)

Shopping can be exhausting in a big city. This clinic offers reflexology and calf-massage sessions for women. The staff are led by a UK-trained massage therapist, so phone bookings aren't a problem. It's conveniently located just off Aoyama-dōri.
✉ Minato-ku, Aoyama 3-13-1, Kobayashi Bldg, 6F ☎ 3470 9855
🚇 Chiyoda line to Omote-sandō, exit B2
🕐 Wed-Mon 11am-9pm, Sun 10am-8pm
💲 ¥5000-10,000

Roppongi Oriental Studio (9, D4)

First fusion cuisine, now fusion massage. A pleasant mix of Western-style techniques and Shiatsu at this place, popular with women but catering to both sexes, on Gaien-higashi-dōri.
✉ Minato-ku, Roppongi, 5-18-20, Roppongi Five Bldg, Rm 301
☎ 3586 1329 🚇 Hibiya line to Roppongi, exit 3
🕐 10am-9pm 💲 ¥5000

Shou Salon (6, C3)

Splendid essential-oil massage in relaxed surroundings, off Omote-sandō. All staff are bilingual.
✉ Shibuya-ku, Jingūmae 4-18-8
☎ 3470 7109
🚇 Chiyoda line to Omote-sandō, exit A1
🕐 10am-9pm
💲 ¥8500-10,000

Michael Taylor

The calm at the eye of the storm: a group practising t'ai-chi in a city park.

out & about

WALKING TOURS
Van Gogh, Vertigo & Shopping

Take the west exit of Shinjuku station and walk through the underground mall. Head for the Shinjuku post office exit and take the stairs to the right. Ahead of you is the Shinjuku Center building ❶. Take the elevator to the 53rd floor and check out the Toilet Zone (toilets of the future). Across the road is the Yasuda Kaisai-Kaijo building ❷, with the 42nd-floor Tōgō Seiji Art Museum and its ¥5 billion Van Gogh's *Sunflowers*. Cross back over the street and walk away from the station. More artwork – photographic – awaits at the Pentax Forum in the Shinjuku Mitsui building ❸, on the next block along Nishi-Shinjuku. Take a left onto Gijidō-dōri till you see the towering Tokyo Metropolitan Government Offices (Tokyo Tochō) ❹, workplace of around 13,000 people. The Citizen's Plaza features shops, restaurants and, er, a blood donation room. The Tochō's free twin observation decks command a marvellous view. Walk south along Tochō-dōri and on the next block stands the eccentric Shinjuku NS building ❺ which has a hollow core. Stand on the ground floor in the 'square' and gaze upward through the transparent roof at the 'sky bridge', 110m overhead. The square also features a 29m pendulum clock, the largest in the world. Take the elevator to the 29th and 30th floors, teeming with restaurants. As you exit the building, turn left onto Tochō-dōri, then left again at One Day's Street. Follow the railway line back to the station. You can walk beneath the tracks and emerge at the multi-store, mega-complex Takashimaya Times Square ❻.

distance 3.5km **duration** 3hrs
▶ **start** 🚇 Yamanote line to Shinjuku, west exit
● **end** 🚇 Shinjuku, new south entrance

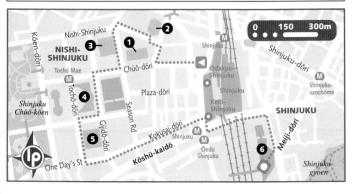

The Pleasure Zone

Surface at the My City exit, in front of the enormous Studio Alta building  video screen. Around dusk is best. Walk east down Shinjuku-dōri to Kinokuniya ❷, with its superb collection of English-language books on Japan. On the left, Isetan ❸ department store has fashionable boutiques, unique souvenirs and Isetan Museum, one of Tokyo's best galleries. Turn left down Yasukuni-dōri to Hanazono-jinja ❹. This shrine has a reputation for

SIGHTS & HIGHLIGHTS

Kinokuniya bookstore (p. 66)
Isetan department store (p. 58)
Golden Gai
Kabukichō

Izzet Keribar

The Pleasure Zone starts here in Shinjuku.

distance 2km
duration 3hrs
▶ **start** 🚉 Yamanote line to Shinjuku, Kabukichō exit
● **end** 🚉 Shinjuku, Kabukichō entrance

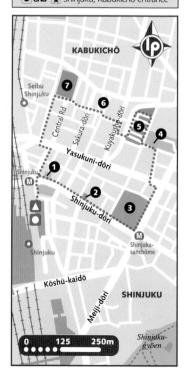

bringing good fortune to business – legitimate and otherwise. Exit onto Golden Gai ❺, a warren of alleyways devoted to small, stand-up watering holes, favourites of Tokyo's bohemian boozers. Drop by before it's redeveloped. Continue in the same direction along the alleyways that run parallel to Yasukuni-dōri and you reach Kabukichō ❻, Tokyo's most notorious 'pleasure district'. Kabukichō has good cheap restaurants. Also 'soaplands' (massage parlours), love hotels, 'no-pants' coffee shops (the waitresses doff their briefs, not the customers), peep shows. You name it… As you walk through neon streets crowded with drunken salarymen, young women wail out invitations to their establishments. Eventually you will arrive at Koma Theatre square ❼, a popular busking spot at night. From here, wander back to to Yasukuni-dōri and take one of the lanes that lead to Shinjuku-dōri and Shinjuku station.

Old Tokyo Town

Exit the Sensō-ji temple through the Hōzō-mon gates ❶. Walk around the edge of the temple grounds and look out for Chingo-dō-ji ❷, a shrine built for *tanuki* (raccoon dogs). Pass the stalls selling kimono, military memorabilia, samurai wigs and other potential souvenirs. Turn right to Hanayashiki Amusement Park ❸, which hasn't changed much since it was built 1853. Nostalgia lovers should check out its Panorama Hall. Take a left, and then another, and you're in Rokku ❹, Asakusa's old cinema district. It is a little down-at-heel nowadays but try to imagine its glamorous heyday. Wander past the local *sembei* (rice cracker) shops to Kaminarimon-dōri and its selection of excellent restaurants. Turn right and cross Kokusai-dōri, cross the street to find the Taikokan Drum Museum ❺ and have a good bash on the displays. You might sidetrack to Raishūken ❻, arguably Tokyo's best *rāmen* shop. Turn right into Kappabashi-dōri ❼ to unearth wax food models, bamboo cooking utensils and *aka-chōchin* (red paper lanterns) that light the back alleys of Tokyo by night. At the end of the street, do a U-turn and head for the building crowned with an enormous model of a chef's head. Turned left at that building and the Tawaramachi subway station is straight ahead.

Get your souvenirs from the shrine.

distance 3km **duration** 2hrs
▶ **start** Ginza line to Asakusa, exit C
● **end** Tawaramachi station, entrance 2

Seaside Stroll

After the 40-minute ride on the Yurikamome monorail, get off at Daiba station and take the main exit. Follow the signs to the futuristic Fuji Television Japan Broadcast Center **1**. Head straight to the observation platform for a view check. Take a right from Fuji TV for Decks Tokyo Beach **2** for shopping and coffee. Backtrack towards Fuji TV, take the first on your right and head for Tokyo's man-made beach. Don't miss Tokyo's very own Statue of Liberty **3** on your right. Keep to the shoreline and when you reach Shiokaze-kōen park turn left. The excellent Museum of Maritime Science **4** is just beyond the park. From here walk in a north-easterly direction, following the monorail line. Look out for the Flame of Liberty statue **5**. You can't miss it – it's the V2 rocket stuck in a pile of cat-litter. It's a short hop on to Palette Town **6**, complete with its own humungous Ferris-wheel. The Renaissance-inspired shopping mall Venus Fort is a good spot for lunch. Next door is the state-of-the-art

SIGHTS & HIGHLIGHTS

Museum of Maritime Science (p. 45)
Venus Fort (p. 39)
Mega Web (p. 44)
Tokyo Big Sight (p. 33)

Fuji Television Japan Broadcast Center

Toyota showroom-cum-amusement-park Mega Web **7**. Cross Dream Bridge to get to the International Exhibition Center (aka 'Tokyo Big Sight') with it's giant saw sculpture out front **8**. The centre looks like an Egyptian pyramid which fell to earth upside-down and the view of Tokyo from the roof is amazing – especially at dusk. Follow the signs back to the monorail station, Kokusai-Tenjijō Seimon, right outside Tokyo Big Sight.

distance 2.5km **duration** 4hrs plus
▶ **start** 🚇 Yurikamome line to Daiba station
● **end** 🚇 Kokusai-Tenjijō Seimon station

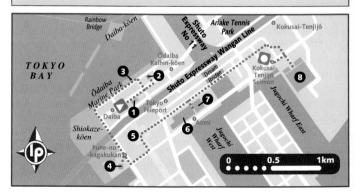

EXCURSIONS
Hakone   (1, C2)

Cable-car rides, an excellent open-air museum, poking around smelly volcanic springs and Ashino-ko lake are the chief pleasures of Hakone. The region is part of the huge Fuji-Hakone-Izu national park, which spreads from Hakone-Yumoto hot springs in the east to Gotemba in the west, and from Mt Fuji in the north down to Atami and the southern coast. Hakone, the town, covers around 25 sq km around Mount Komaga-take (1357m).

It's worth purchasing a *furii passu* or free pass which is valid on the Ōdakyū line from Shinjuku to Hakone-Yumoto and any transport with the Hakone region. Another bonus is the discounts it allows on entry to some sights.

Don't miss the excellent **Hakone Open-Air Art Museum**. It is only 100m south of Chokoku-no-mori station and set in a 30-sq-km park filled with August Rodin and Henry Moore sculptures – perfect for picnics. Take the Sounzan Funicular from the next station, Gōra, up to **Ōwakudani** with its sulphurous hot springs.

From Ōwakudani, the cable car continues on to Tōgendai, the stop for Ashino-ko. This lake is the primary attraction of the area. It's also where you can experience one of the classic views of Mt Fuji. There are ferries across the lake to **Moto-Hakone** stop. Grab a bite to eat here and check out the distinctive red *torii* (gate) of **Hakone-jinja** shrine, rising from the water. The shrine itself is nothing special, but the effect is quite evocative.

A cloud drifts across the face of Mt Fuji (3776m), as seen from Lake Ashino-ko

Kamakura   (1, C3)

Kamakura had a spell of glory as the nation's capital from 1192 to 1333, and its wealth of notable temples and shrines make it one of Tokyo's most rewarding day trips. Relaxing walks and a peace that is hard to come by in central Tokyo, are part of its appeal.

The city's attractions are spread out in an inverted horseshoe shape around Kamakura station, the most distant less than 2km away. All can easily be seen by walking, augmented with the occasional bus ride. The best route is to start at Kita-Kamakura station and visit temples between there and Kamakura on foot. Temples are well signposted in English and Japanese.

Tōkei-ji is famous for its grounds as much as for the temple itself. Women were once officially recognised as divorced if they spent three years as nuns here. Explore **Kenchō-ji**, Kamakura's most important Zen temple with its enormous temple bell. This temple and its surrounding gardens are well-kept and still in use as a centre for Buddhist meditation and study.

The ornate **Tsurugaoka Hachiman-gū shrine** makes for a dramatic contrast to the Zen temple. It's dedicated to Hachiman, the god of war. The **National Treasure Museum** provides a unique opportunity to see Kamakura art; most of it is kept away in the temples. The highlight is the 11.4m-tall, 850-tonne **Daibutsu**, or Great Buddha, inspired by, but artistically superior to, the Great Buddha in Nara. Its home was washed away by a tsunami, or tidal wave, in 1495.

INFORMATION

50km south of Tokyo

- 🚆 Yokosuka line from Tokyo station to Kamakura, 55mins; train (one way) ¥890
- ☎ 0467 22 0753 National Treasure Museum
- ℹ TIC at east exit of Kamakura station (☎ 0467 22 3350, 9am-5pm)
- 🕐 temples & shrines 9am-4.30pm; National Treasure Museum 9am-4pm (closed Mon); Great Buddha 7am-5.30pm
- 💲 Tōkei-ji temple ¥200; Kenchō-ji temple ¥300; National Treasure Museum ¥150; Great Buddha ¥200
- ✘ restaurants opposite Kamakura station

John McInnes

Daibutsu (Great Buddha) of Kamakura

Mt Fuji   (1, C1)

Even though it's one of the world's most famous mountains, the 3776m-high mountain is notoriously reclusive, often hidden by cloud.

Views are best in winter and early spring, when the skies are clear and the snow cap adds to the scene. In summer the view is generally poor because it disappears behind the heat-haze and pollution from the factories that lie to the south.

If you're intent on taking a peek, the bus from Shinjuku stops at the Fifth Station on the northern side. The height at this point is 2393m. It isn't really a 'station' – just a carpark where climbers start from. You can then at least boast you've climbed *on* Mt Fuji.

From here, there are excellent views to the west across Lake Motso-ko (portrayed on the ¥5000 note) and the Sea of Trees (a favourite spot for suicides and disposal of murder victims). To the north it's possible to see Lake Kawaguchi-ko and to the east Lake Yamanako-ko.

Climbing Mt Fuji

If you ponder an ascent of Fuji-san it might pay to find out more about it before you head off. The climbing season is in July and August and outside of this the weather may permit a climb but transportation services are irregular. Climbing in mid-winter is only for experienced mountaineers. Mt Fuji is high enough for altitude sickness and oxygen is for sale at the top. The weather is changeable so take clothing suitable for every type. Most climbers leave Tokyo at around 10pm and do the trek overnight. Arriving at the top at dawn ensures the sunrise experience of a lifetime.

Bob Charlton

Nikkō   (1, A3)

There's a hoary, oft-trotted-out Japanese adage – 'Don't say *kekko* till you've seen Nikkō'. *'Kekko'* means fine or splendid. Well, for once the hype is true. Nikkō, and its showpiece **Tōshō-gū shrine**, is unmissable. You'll need a full day and an early start from Tokyo, but this is a foray out of the city you shouldn't miss, no matter how short your stay. It's a 30-minute walk or short bus ride straight up the hill from the train station to the shrine area. There's definitely a day's worth of exploring here. On the way to the shrine area, take a look at the arched bridge, **Shin-kyō-bashi** currently closed for repairs and due to reopen in 2002.

At the heart of Nikkō's shrine-filled mountain enclave is Tōshō-gū shrine. The mausoleum of Shōgun Tokugawa Ieyasu is 'pure 17th-century Disneyland', according to British art historian Gordon Miller. Ieyasu's shrine is crowded with detail. Every single centimetre has been used to remind you of its creator's munificence and power. Dragons, lions and peacocks jostle with gods and demi-gods among the glimmering gold-leaf and red lacquerwork. This is as far as you can get from the minimalism of Zen architecture, but don't let this put you off – Tōshō-gū remains a grand sensory roller-coaster ride.

Don't miss **Rinnō-ji temple** and its **Sambutsu-dō** (Three Buddha Hall) with a trio of huge, remarkable gold-lacquered images; and the **Hōbutsu-den** (Treasure Hall), featuring beautiful Buddhist artwork and a lovely Edo-period garden **Shōyō-en**.

A popular spot to eat is **Hippari Dako** which specialises in *yakitori* and is run by the very friendly Miki-san. It's on your left as you walk towards the shrine compound, just before Shin-kyō-bashi, identifiable by the large kite hanging above the entrance. It closes in the early evening, so don't be late!

INFORMATION
110km north of Tokyo
- 🚃 Tōbu Nikkō line from Asakusa to Nikkō, 2hrs then bus No 1, 2, 3 or 4 up hill to Shin-kyō-bashi bus stop; last train back at 7.42pm
- ℹ️ TIC Tōbu Nikkō station
- 🕐 shrines & temples 8am-4pm
- 💲 train ¥2740; bus ¥190; main shrines & temples combination ticket ¥1350
- 🍴 Hippari Dako (☎ 0288 53 2933, till 7pm)

Detail from Tōshō-gū shrine

ORGANISED TOURS

If you're visiting Tokyo for a limited amount of time or simply can't face the crowds and noise of public transport, consider taking an organised tour of the major sights. The major tour companies listed below have pick-up points city-wide.

Hato Bus (12, E4)

The distinctive yellow tour buses have been whisking foreigners around Tokyo for decades. Day and night tours, some including dinner at a sukiyaki restaurant. Perfect for the lazy tourist. The name means, oddly, Pigeon Bus.

✉ Tokyo station, Marunouchi exit
☎ 3435 6081
[e] www.hatobus.co.jp/ english ⏲ daily
$ Panoramic Tour ¥9800 incl lunch

Mr Oka

The eponymous cheery old cove guides you through Old Yamanote, Kanda and Asakusa. Half- and full-day options and customised tours available. Lunches, admission and subway fees are extra. Call after 7pm to arrange where to meet.

☎ 0422 51 7673
[e] www.mroka .homestead.com
⏲ by appointment
$ from ¥2000/person

Tramming It

Tokyo has a solitary tram service still in operation. There used to be an extensive tram system across the city but as car ownership became popular in the 1960s and 70s, trams just got in the way. The Toden Arakawa tram line doesn't really go anywhere special, but it passes through a couple of areas that haven't (yet) been claimed by redevelopment. It runs from **Waseda** (west side of Tokyo) to **Minowabashi** (east Tokyo).

The best place to get on is at the **Zōshigaya cemetery** (2, E5; Yūrakuchō line to Higashi-Ikebukuro). The cemetery is the resting place of Lafcadio Hearn, remarkable cosmopolitan chronicler of everyday Meiji Japan, and of his contemporary, the immensely popular writer Natsume Sōseki. From here the tram trundles east past **Sunshine City** and through **Ōtsuka** and **Sugamo**, passing a number of temples. After Ikebukuro, the tram is mostly off-road, winding through interesting residential areas.

Odakyū Q-Tours

(4, C3) Specialises in tours to Kamakura, Mt Fuji and Hakone. Meet at Odakyū Sightseeing Service Center, near the west exit of Odakyū-Shinjuku station. An English guidebook is included. There's an office in the Hotel Century Hyatt.

✉ Shinjuku-ku, Odakyū-Shinjuku 1F
☎ 5321 7887
⏲ 8am-6pm
$ ¥6800-9500

Sunrise Tours (3, L7)

Offers longer trips outside the city, including Mt Fuji and Hakone, Nikkō and Kamakura. Best though is their Geisha Tour, which includes dinner. Starts at Hamamatsuchō Bus Terminal, drop off in Ginza.

✉ Shinagawa-ku, Higashi-Shinagawa, 2-3-11
☎ 5796 5454
⏲ daily from 8am; Geisha Tour 4.30-7pm
$ ¥6800-18,800

Taking a taxi in Tokyo is a treat.

Oliver Strewe

shopping

As any Tokyoite will happily tell you, you are what you buy. Shopping defines this city. The sacred palaces in contemporary Tokyo's consumer culture are the enormous, opulent *depāto*, or department stores. They are pervasive, irresistible. It's impossible to leave Tokyo without having bought *something*, be it a radio-controlled robotic dog or an early Edo-period teapot. Don't try to resist. You can't.

Shopping Areas

Searching for good shopping in Tokyo is akin to searching for sand in the Gobi. It's everywhere. Yet there are several notable areas where rampant commercialism has saturated the environment like a summer typhoon.

Akihabara is manga and electronics. Shinjuku competes on even terms for both and offers even more with Takashimaya Times Square – more a commercial space-station-come-to-earth

Duty Free

Duty free shopping is only possible at Narita Airport and other international gateways. However authorised tax-free outlets in the major shopping areas cater to tourists, in English. You can be exempted from the 5% *shōhizei* consumption tax if your purchase comes to more than ¥10,000. However on items such as video and electronic goods, the discount stores in Akihabara and Shinjuku may be cheaper anyway.

than a store. Shibuya responds with flashy teen trash, and artsy trendiness. Ginza plays the high-price status card. Aoyama, boutique chic to the nth degree turns up its collar, and its nose…and the shopping war rages on.

Only Asakusa, proud of its rough old roots sits back…then lets you have it with both materialistic barrels, in the form of Nakamise-dōri, where history is carefully packaged and resold as papier-mache dolls, kimono…We reiterate, IT IS USELESS TO RESIST.

John McInnes

Sales are frequent and regular: just don't be a victim of last year's fashion.

DEPARTMENT STORES & MALLS

Shopping in a Tokyo department store is a unique experience. If you arrive at opening time you will receive an elaborate welcome from the staff. The atmosphere is electric at times – especially during sales and on public holidays. Basement floors are reserved for food, the top floors usually have a selection of restaurants to choose from and in between, everything else. Enjoy.

Isetan (4, B5)
Long identified as *the* Tokyo department store, Isetan's window displays are always eye-catching if not downright bizarre. There's a customer service department on the 7th floor that provides English-speaking guides.
✉ **Shinjuku-ku, Shinjuku 3-14-1**
☎ **3352 1111**
Ⓜ **Marunouchi line to Shinjuku-sanchōme, exits B3, B4 & B5**
🚉 **Yamanote line to Shinjuku, Lumine 2 exit**
🕐 **Thurs-Tues 10am-7.30pm**

Marui (4, B5)
Good spot to pick up inexpensive but good quality youth-oriented clothing, as long as you're Japanese-sized. Take heart shoppers, Japanese youth are getting a lot bigger. This place debuted with easy credit lines aimed at the high disposable income youth market and parlayed it into huge success. You can't throw a coat-hanger in Shinjuku without hitting a Marui.
✉ **Shinjuku-ku, Shinjuku 3-18-1**
☎ **3354 0101**
Ⓜ **Marunouchi & Toei Shinjuku lines to Shinjuku-sanchōme, exits A2 & A3**
🕐 **10am-8pm**

Matsuya (12, F5)
Great for foreign visitors, Matsuya has the full works with packaging and international shipping service, tax-exemption assistance and useful, if haphazard, in-store English-speaking guides.
✉ **Chūō-ku, Ginza 3-6-1**
☎ **3567 1211**
Ⓜ **Ginza, Marunouchi & Hibiya lines to Ginza, exits A12 & A13**
🕐 **10.30am-8pm**

Mitsukoshi (12, G5)
An upmarket goodie-filled leviathan of a store in the heart of Nihonbashi. Tokyo's oldest department store was originally modelled on that London bastion of commerce, Harrods. The tax-exemption section is in the basement.
✉ **Chūō-ku, Nihonbashi-muromachi 1-4-1** ☎ **3241 3311**

Tokyoites celebrate the changing of the season with the ubiquitous 'spring jacket'.

Oliver Strewe

 Hanzōmon & Ginza
lines to Mitsukoshimae,
exits A2, A3, A5, A7 & A8
 10am-7pm

Seibu Loft (5, C3)
Aimed at 18-35 year olds,
Loft offers an enormous
range of goodies that most
sensible people would
never even *consider* shop-
ping for. Thus it's guaran-
teed you'll spend up.
Especially the whacky nov-
elty goods on the 5th floor.
 Shibuya-ku,
Udagawachō 21-1
 3462 3807
 Ginza & Hanzōmon
lines to Shibuya,
exits 6 & 7
 Yamanote line to
Shibuya, east exit
 Sun-Wed 10am-8pm,
Thurs-Sat 10am-9pm

**Sunshine City Alpa
(2, C5)** Ikebukuro's shopping mecca is not as trendy
as its Shibuya and Shinjuku
competitors, nor is it quite
so crowded. And you're still
deluged with shopping possibilities. There is also a
good aquarium and a hyp-
notic car showroom on site.
 Toshima-ku,
Higashi-Ikebukuro 3-1-3
 3989 3331
 Marunouchi &
Yūrakuchō lines to
Ikebukuro, exits C4, C7,
C8, 1b & 2a
 10am-8pm

Takashimaya (12, C5)
The department store that
specialises in delivering
expensive gifts during the
New Year and mid-summer
gift-giving seasons, this is
another cornucopia of
temptations in Nihonbashi.
The branch in the Times
Square complex in Shinjuku
claims to be the world's
largest department store.

Tokyo's own slice of the Big Apple

Both are stuffed with boutiques, department stores,
restaurants and game cen-
tres, making it the perfect
refuge during a typhoon. In
fact, you could probably
live there.
 Chūō-ku,
Nihonbashi 2-4-1
 3211 4111
 Ginza & Tōzai lines
to Nihonbashi, exits B1
& B2 10am-7pm

Tōkyū Hands (5, C2)
Ostensibly a do-it-yourself
store, it is actually a comprehensive collection of
everything you might want
to bring home, from
sewing repair kits to chain-
saws, hand-crafted wire
tofu-tongs and scale rep-
licas of the Enola Gay. The
Godzilla section is a must.
Also branches in Ikebukuro
and Takashimaya Times
Square.
 Shibuya-ku,
Udagawachō 12-18
 5489 5111
 Ginza & Hanzōmon
lines to Shibuya,
exits 6 & 7
 Yamanote line to
Shibuya, east exit
 Tues-Sun 10am-8pm

Comparison shopping is essential.

CLOTHING

Tokyoites have long spent copious wads of cash on how they look – it's very important to look right in this city of style. The city is fashion mad, from hip-hop street wear to clubber chic, to the high-price designer brands of Aoyama. You can't fail to find something you like and you can bet no-one will be wearing *that* when you get back home. As with anywhere else on the globe, department stores usually have international and local designer-label boutiques in their clothing sections.

Comme Des Garcons
(6, D5) Rei Kawakubo hit the yuppie fashion vein when she pioneered the matt-black designs that propelled her to international fashion stardom in the early 80s. Her enduring trademark remains matt-black chic. This Aoyama wonder is her snooty flagship store.
✉ Minato-ku, Minami-Aoyama 5-2-1
Ⓣ Ginza, Hanzōmon & Chiyoda lines to Omote-sandō, exit A5
🕐 11am-8pm

Hanae Mori (6, B5)
Much beloved by the French (as indeed is Kawakubo), Hanae Mori's 'European classic' style is

Issey Miyake: taking risks in Aoyama.

also much emulated, but her real success lies in her adulation amongst hordes of *ojō-sama*, the conservative well-brought-up daughters of the Tokyo rich.
✉ Minato-ku, Kita-Aoyama 3-6-1
☎ 3423 1448
Ⓣ Ginza, Hanzōmon, Chiyoda lines to Omote-sandō, exit A1
🕐 11am-7pm

Hysteric Glamour
(6, D1) Fabulous tongue-in-cheek designer fashions for well-off youths or their indulgent parents. The toddler range is totally hilarious, characterised by the snotty cartoon infant sticking her tongue out at the world.

This is the ultimate in designer punk for tots!
✉ Shibuya-ku, Jingūmae 6-23-2
☎ 3409 7227
Ⓣ Chiyoda line to Meiji-jingūmae, exits 1 & 4
🚃 Yamanote line to Harajuku, Omote-sandō exit 🕐 11am-8pm

Issey Miyake (6, D5)
Japan's true fashion anarchist, Issey Miyake, has never been afraid to experiment with odd styles and peculiar materials, yet somehow his clothes always managed to look and feel tremendous. His current line of jackets resemble ultra-chic, slimmed-down Michelin-tyre men. This Aoyama showroom looks

Laforet's street art ads

more like a gallery than a shop.

✉ **Minato-ku, Minami-Aoyama 3-18-11** ☎ **3423 1407, 3423 1408** 🚇 **Ginza, Hanzōmon, Chiyoda lines to Omote-sandō, exit A4** ⏱ **10am-8pm**

Laforet (6, C2)

It's rampant commercialism decked out as modern art. It's a teenage fashion 'happening'. It's a post-modern shopping mall masquerading as a museum. It's Tokyo youth incarnate. Whatever Laforet is, it is really quite spectacular. Have your abstract expressionism and wear it too. The fourth floor

The Etiquette of Shopping

When you pay a cashier for an item, look for the rectangular, plastic dish somewhere on the counter. This is where you place the money. Don't try to put it in the cashier's hand. It's okay to add coins to make the change simpler. So if the item you are buying costs ¥250, put down ¥1050, if you're familiar enough with the currency. The cashier will then place the change in the dish and move it towards you. Bow slightly and leave.

Lapnet Ship is, you guessed it, a clothing store.

✉ **Shibuya-ku, Jingūmae 1-11-6** ☎ **5411 3330** 🚉 **Yamanote line to Harajuku, Omote-sandō exit** ⏱ **11am-8pm**

JEWELLERY & ACCESSORIES

Mikimoto Pearl (12, G4) This is the most famous of Tokyo's pearl shops. It was founded by the pearl king himself, Mikimoto Kokichi, the man who first developed the cultured pearl, and it has been running since 1899. Mikimoto Pearl is located in glamorous Ginza, right next door to Wakō department store and opposite Mitsukoshi.

✉ **Chūō-ku, Ginza 5-5-4** ☎ **3535 4611** 🚇 **Ginza, Marunouchi & Hibiya lines to Ginza, exit B5** ⏱ **9.30am-6.30pm**

Tasaki Shinju (12, G5) This store is owned by Mikimoto's chief rival who is perhaps more experimental in his use of the gems. Many consider Tasaki Shinju not *quite* as classy as Mikimoto. Still this is a hugely popular store, with some startling looking pieces of jewellery. There is also a branch in Akasaka.

✉ **Chūō-ku, Ginza 5-7-5** ☎ **3289 1111** 🚇 **Ginza, Marunouchi & Hibiya lines to Ginza, exits A1 & A2** ⏱ **10.30am-7.30pm**

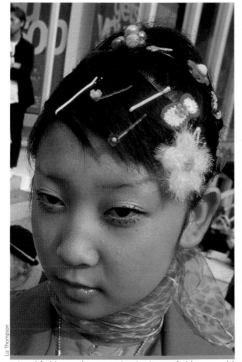

Liz Thompson

Local fashion acolytes – cool, calm & not afraid to wear it!

MARKETS

Despite the fascination of the giant department stores and shopping complexes, there's nothing quite like getting out onto the Tokyo streets at one of its markets.

Ameya yoko-chō

(10, E3) Thriving daily market that transformed itself from a post-war den of black-market skulduggery into the nearest thing Tokyo has to an Asian street market. The city's African, Asian and Indian communities have joined the throng, so you can pick up Thai curry mix along with your *kimchee* pickles and dried squid. There's also something of an illicit trade in counterfeit watches and bags.
⊠ Taitō-ku, Ueno 4

🚇 Ginza & Hibiya lines to Ueno, exit 5b
🚃 Yamanote line to Ueno, Hirokoji exit
🕐 10am-8pm

Hanazono-jinja Antique Market

(4, B5) This place bills itself as an antique market, ie, much the same stuff as at the flea markets, but with higher prices. It's right on the edge of Kabukichō.
⊠ Shinjuku-ku, Shinjuku 5-17-3
☎ 3200 3093
🚇 Marunouchi line to Shinjuku-sanchōme, exit C6 🕐 Sun 7am-5pm

Heiwajima Kotto Ichi Antique Fair

(3, P6) This huge three-day antique market usually takes place five times each year. Every-thing from top-class ceramics to samurai armour to postage stamps.
⊠ Ōta-ku, Heiwajima 6-1-1, Heiwajima Tokyo Ryūtsū Bldg Centre, 2F
☎ 3980 8228
🚃 Tokyo Monorail to Ryūtsū Centre, main exit 🕐 1-3 Mar, 3-5 May, 28-30 June, 13-15 Sept & 20-22 Dec; 10am-6pm

Nogi-jinja flea market

(9, A2) This cheery market takes place once a month and is not as crowded as others. It's just around the corner from the Asia Centre of Japan.
⊠ Minato-ku, Akasaka 8-11-27 ☎ 3478 3001
🚇 Chiyoda line to Nogizaka, exit 1
🕐 2nd Sun each month, 5am-4pm

Tōgō-jinja flea market

(6, B2) A great little flea market, right in the heart of swinging Harajuku, that constantly produces interesting finds.
⊠ Shibuya-ku, Jingū-mae 1-5-3 ☎ 3403 3591 🚃 Yamanote line to Harajuku, Takeshita-guchi exit 🕐 1st, 4th & 5th Sun each month, 6am-3pm

Flea Market Finds

Things to look for include old kimonos, scrolls, pottery, Chinese snuff bottles, old Japanese postcards, military memorabilia, antique toys and costume jewellery. A Tokyo flea market is the only place where it is acceptable to bargain. But be polite.

Mixing treasure & trash at Nogi-jinja shrine flea market.

John Ashburne

CAMERAS & ELECTRONICS

While the range of electronic products is astounding, many products are only for the domestic market. It may be impossible to have repairs done once you return home. While Akihabara (Electric Town) is notorious for bargains, some say the big stores in Ikebukuro are just as good. Shinjuku has the most competitive prices for cameras and film. Make sure the voltages of electronic products will be compatible (p. 113) with that of your country. Some stores have tax-free floors for non-residents.

Bic Camera (2, B3)

Bic Camera claims to be the cheapest camera store in Japan, a claim hotly disputed by Yodobashi and Sakuraya camera stores. Its big bargain bins of film that is approaching its expiry date are good value – the merchandise is fine. There's also a branch in Shibuya.

✉ **Toshima-ku, Higashi-Ikebukuro 1-41**
☎ **3988 0002**
🚇 **Marunouchi line to Ikebukuro, exits 23, 29 & 30** ◷ **10am-8pm**

Laox (13, B9)

Huge chain of stores selling discounted electrical equipment. Prices are competitive, but make sure that infra-red tofu blender is compatible with your home voltage before you lug it on the plane.
✉ **Chiyoda-ku, Soto-Kanda 1-2-9**
☎ **3255 9041**
🚆 **Yamanote line to Akihabara, Electric Town exit**
◷ **10am-7.30pm**

Sakuraya Camera (4, B4)

Yodobashi Camera's chief rival offers much the same as others here and at similar prices. You'll find some good deals here but like anywhere, comparison shopping is essential.
✉ **Shinjuku-ku, Shinjuku 3-17-2**
☎ **3354 3636**
🚇 **Marunouchi line to Shinjuku, exits B7, B8 & B9** ◷ **10am-8pm**

Softmap (13, A9)

A decade or so ago, no-one had ever heard of Softmap. Now it rules the cut-price computer world with a fist of steel. Or silicon. Crafty marketing, ruthless discounting and a staff of techno-nerds, has seen the company sprout no less than 16 branches in Akihabara alone. Each one specialises in new and used Macs, PCs and other odd hybrids. All cyberlife is here.
✉ **Chiyoda-ku, Kami-Kanda 3-14-10**
☎ **5609 6597**

🚆 **Yamanote line to Akihabara, Electric Town exit**
◷ **Mon-Sat 10.30am-8pm, Sun 10am-7pm**

T Zone Computers (13, A9)

T Zone is no longer the biggest player in the Akihabara computer war but it still has the best selection of machines with English operating systems and software. There's a branch in Shinjuku.
✉ **Chiyoda-ku, Soto-Kanda 4-3-3**
☎ **3257 2650**
🚆 **Yamanote line to Akihabara, Electric Town exit**
◷ **Sun-Thurs 10.30am-7pm, Fri-Sat 10.30am-7.30pm**

Yodobashi Camera (4, D3)

One of Tokyo's most famous camera stores, this emporium stocks anything from digital cameras to second-hand enlargers. Prices are very competitive. Passport ID is required to have the consumption tax waived.
✉ **Shinjuku-ku, Nishi-Shinjuku 1-11-1**
☎ **3346 1010**
🚇 **Toei Shinjuku line to Shinjuku, exit 5**
🚇 **Chūō line to Shinjuku, Minami-guchi & south exits**
◷ **9.30am-9pm**

Your only duty is to your credit card.

DUTY FREE AKIHABARA

John Ashburne

ART & ANTIQUES

Fuji Torii (6, D3)
This reliable antique dealer has been in the business since 1948 and stocks everything from exquisite *kutani* ceramics to inexpensive modern woodblock prints. They have an especially good selection of *byobu* screens.
✉ Shibuya ku, Jingūmae 6-1-10
☎ 3400 2777
Ⓜ Chiyoda line to Meiji-jingūmae, exit 4
🕐 Wed-Mon 11am-6pm

Inachu Lacquerware (8, D4)
A renowned lacquerware shop from Ishikawa, specialising in that area's prized and pricey *wajima-nuri*. Strictly for those who want the genuine item and are prepared to pay for it. Prices start at ¥30,000.
✉ Minato-ku, Akasaka 1-5-2 ☎ 3582 4451
Ⓜ Ginza & Namboku lines to Tameike-sannō, exit 9 🕐 Mon-Sat 10am-6pm

Japan Sword (12, K1)
Highly respected dealer in swords, with much experience in helping foreign tourists choose the right weapon for their taste. And budget. Priciest and spookiest are the *tameshi-giri* blades that have been 'used on humans'.
✉ Minato-ku, Toranomon 3-8-1, Mori Bldg
☎ 3434 4321
🇪 www.japansword.co.jp Ⓜ Hibiya line to Kamiyacho, exit 3
🕐 Mon-Fri 9.30am-6pm, Sat 9.30am-5pm

Japan Traditional Crafts Center (6, B5)
The craft centre, on the corner of Aoyama-dōri and Killer-dōri, has changing displays of Japanese crafts and other good-quality items for sale. Nearby, hidden among the trendy boutiques on Kotto-dōri are some 30 antique shops. They're in a side street to the left of Aoyama-dōri if you are walking in the direction of Shibuya.
✉ Minato-ku, Minami-Aoyama 3-1-1
☎ 3403 2460
Ⓜ Ginza line to Gaienmae, exit 1
🕐 Fri-Wed 10am-6pm

Ohya Shobō (3, F7)
Splendid musty old bookstore specialising in *ukiyo-e* prints and ancient maps. You could get lost in here for hours and the friendly staff can help you find whatever particular piece of antiquated trivia your heart desires.
✉ Chiyoda-ku, Kanda Jimbōchō 1-1
☎ 3291 0062
🇪 www.abaj.gr.jp/ohyashobo/index-j.htm
Ⓜ Toei Shinjuku, Toei Mita & Hanzōmon lines to Jimbōchō, exit A7
🕐 Mon-Sat 10am-6pm

Shipping Home your Spoils
By far the simplest, most economical way to ship home your souvenir booty is using the services of the **Tokyo International Post Office** (12, C3). Sending parcels overseas from Japan can be as much as 30% cheaper than airmail with Surface Airlift (SAL), and only takes a week longer. Note that post offices conveniently sell different sized cardboard boxes, which allows you to pack and send on the spot. Larger department stores can also arrange international postage.

Private freight couriers are loathe to ship materials abroad for non-resident non-Japanese, as packages come under complex taxation and import restrictions. The exception is **Sagawa Kyūbin** (☎ 3699 3377) who will not only handle the paperwork, but they'll pick up your package from the hotel. You'll need to show your passport.

John Ashburne

Japanese fan: souvenir cliche or cultural treasure?

On Sundays (6, B4)

Avant-garde art in the form of funky stationery and trendy-sometimes-comical postcards in this fascinating shop tucked on to the side of the Watari Museum of Contemporary Art. There's also a marvellous selection of T-shirts, CD ROMs and books on photography, architecture and fine art.

✉ Shibuya-ku, Jingūmae 3-7-6
☎ 3470 1424
🚇 Ginza line to Gaienmae, exit 2
🕐 Tues-Sun 11am-8pm

Oriental Bazaar (6,D3)

This shop has a wide-ranging selection of antiques and tourist items, some at very reasonable prices. Items for sale that would make great souvenirs include fans, folding screens, pottery, porcelain and kimonos. Good one-stop shopping. The branch at Narita airport opens at 7.30am for last-minute suit-of-armour purchases.

✉ Shibuya-ku, Jingūmae 5-9-13
☎ 3400 3933

🚇 Chiyoda line to Meiji-jingūmae, exit 4
🕐 Fri-Wed 9.30am-6.30pm

Satomi Building (2, E2)

The locals call it this, but its real name is Tokyo Ko-mingu Kotto Kan (Tokyo Antique Hall). It's a collection of around two dozen small antique shops, many specialising in items such as ceramics, ukiyo-e, masks, paintings and small statues from Japan and nearby Asian countries. Prices and quality vary.

✉ Toshima-ku, Minami-Ikebukuro 3-9-5
☎ 3980 8228
🚃 Yamanote line to Ikebukuro, east exit
🕐 Mon-Sat 10am-6pm

Tolman Collection (3, L6)

Fine selection of exquisite antiques at suitably exquisite prices in this long-established, highly regarded establishment down in Daimon.

✉ Minato-ku, Shiba-Daimon 2-2-18
☎ 3434 1300
📧 www.tolmatokyo.com
🚇 Toei Ōedo line to Daimon, exit A3
🕐 Wed-Mon 11am-7pm

Samurai going cheap! Own your very own samurai!

BOOKS & MUSIC

HMV (5, C3)
His Master's Voice challenges the domination of Tower Records. Its smaller scale makes for a far more relaxing browse than in the frenetic tower. Fancy video previews too.
✉ Shibuya-ku, Udagawachō 24-1
☎ 5458 3411
Ⓣ Ginza & Hanzōmon lines to Shibuya, exits 3 & 6 ⏰ 10am-10pm

Kinokuniya (4, D4)
This annexe branch surpasses the main store with its variety and depth of titles in English. The 'Books on Japan' section is a great place to pick up visual material to substantiate the crazy stories you'll tell when you get home.
✉ Shinjuku-ku, Sendagaya 5-24-2, Takashimaya Times Square, Annex Bldg
☎ 5361 3301
Ⓣ Chūō line to Shinjuku, south exit
⏰ 10am-8pm (closed one Wed/month)

Sekaido Stationery (4, B4) Tokyo is manga mad, and animated characters from Sailor Moon to Pokemon to Humungo the Wolfman (OK that last one's made up) dot the landscape like a visual blight. Or blessing, depending on your viewpoint. Sekaido stocks a vast array of *anime* from the strokes-of-genius to the brown-paper wrapper. Happy browsing.
✉ Shinjuku-ku, Shinjuku 3-1-1
☎ 3356 1515
Ⓣ Marunouchi &

An eyeful of the latest manga

John Ashburne

Toei Shinjuku lines to Shinjuku-sanchōme, exit C1
⏰ 10am-7.30pm

Tower Records (5, C3)
Tokyo's largest music store (and that's saying something). Despite its size, this place still gets packed to the gunwales. Still this is the best place in town to find that rare 'Frank Fish & the Fins' CD, you've always wanted. If you can't get it here, you can't get it anywhere.
✉ Shibuya-ku, Jinnan 1-22-14
☎ 3496 3661
Ⓣ Ginza & Hanzōmon lines to Shibuya, exit 7
⏰ 10am-10pm

Virgin Megastore (4, C5) The Branson empire reaches Tokyo with this flagship store. While it's much the same as its sister stores around the world, it's a relatively small outlet so staff are helpful and there's a fair selection of home-grown music to sample. There's also a branch in Ikebukuro.
✉ Shinjuku-ku, Shinjuku 3-30-16, Marui Fashion Bdg, B1F
☎ 5952 5600
Ⓣ Toei Shinjuku & Marunouchi lines to Shinjuku-sanchōme, exit A4 Ⓡ Yamanote line to Shinjuku, Kabukichō exit
⏰ 11am-8pm

Manga? Anime? What's the Difference?

Anywhere else in the world comic books are the domain of hormonally explosive teenage boys, but in Japan there are **manga** (comic books) for almost every age group and taste. There's the extremely popular **shonen** (young boys) genre that has the predictable tales of righting wrongs and getting the girl. These are balanced by **shojo** (young girls), light-hearted comics often featuring complex human relationships, such as *Sailor Moon*. For more mature readers, **shonen-ai** (boys' love) captures a female audience wanting to see graphic male homosexuality. The much publicised **hentai** (pervert) genre features graphic sexual or horror material including full nudity, though it represents only a fraction of the market.

Originally inspired by early Disney animated movies, manga remained uncensored throughout the 1950s and 60s while outside Japan comics were scrutinised and forced to remove sex and violence from their pages. In Japan, manga flourished by expanding its audience beyond children and teenagers, though the adult content still leaves many Western readers blushing. Modern manga covers subjects as diverse as sport, *benkyo* (study, including international finance) , and romance stories such as *Ah! my Goddess*. Manga is available from vending machines for easy train reading or for the real connoisseurs there's the semi-annual *Komikku Māketto* (Comic Market) in Tokyo.

The success of manga has extended to animation or anime as its known in Japanese. Television series such as 'Astroboy', 'Pokemon' and 'Neon Genesis Evangelion' have made a splash internationally. With the advent of computer-generated technology, animation has become more elaborate and cheaper allowing longer movie-length anime. *Mononoke Hime* (1997), a mythical tale of a wolf princess saving her civilisation from the evils of technology, used computer-generated technology extensively and received international release with a dubbed version featuring the voices of Hollywood heavy hitters Billy Bob Thornton, Minnie Driver and Claire Danes. Another experimental anime is the late night TV favourite *Eat Man* with a title hero who eats metal and swills petrol to build machinery in his body. There is no technological cure for his indigestion.

George Dunford

SPECIALIST STORES

Axis Building (9, C5)
This complex in Roppongi is an excellent place to catch up on some of Japan's most innovative interior design. Of the 20 or so retail shops and galleries, highlights are Kisso, specialising in ceramics and Yoshikin for beautifully crafted, inexpensive kitchenware. Their knives make a splendid present.
✉ **Minato-ku, Roppongi 5-17-1**
☎ **3587 2781**
🚇 **Hibiya line to Roppongi, exit 3**
🕐 **Mon-Sat 11am-7pm**

Illums (2, C2)
Trolls and designer teapots galore at this sleek emporium of Scandinavian homewares on the first and second floors of Seibu Ikebukuro's East building. Not sure what an Illum is though.
✉ **Toshima-ku, Minami-Ikebukuro 1-28-1** ☎ **5992 8678**
🚉 **Yamanote line to Ikebukuro, west exit**
🕐 **Mon-Sat 10am-9pm**

International Arcade (12, G4) Not one arcade but two. Part 1 is on the Uchisaiwaichō side of the rail tracks, Part 2 the Yūrakuchō side, near Ginza. Both are a conglomeration of stores specialising in 'Japanese' souvenirs – everything from DVD players to 'I luv Tokyo' T-shirts. English is spoken, tax refunds are available and all major credit cards are accepted. In reality there's not much quality stuff amongst the tourist tat,

but it *is* convenient. SI Brothers are a cut above the rest.
✉ **Chiyoda-ku, Yūrakuchō 2-1-1**
☎ **3591 9826, 3501 4012** 🚇 **Marunouchi & Hibiya lines to Ginza, exits A1 & C1**
🕐 **9.30am-6.30pm**

In The Room (2, B1)
Part of Marui department store, but a few blocks down from the main store in Ikebukuro. Everything from furniture to coffee cups to kitchen appliances. The interior design of the store is a treat in itself.
✉ **Toshima-ku, Ikebukuro**
🚉 **Yamanote line to Ikebukuro, west exit**
🕐 **Mon-Sat 10am-8pm**

Itoya (12, F5)
Itoya has nine floors of every kind of stationery item you can imagine. What's more, it also stocks a comprehensive collection of *washi*, traditional Japanese paper. It's also possible to get things printed or photocopied here.
✉ **Chūō-ku, Ginza 2-7-15**
☎ **3561 8311**
🚇 **Ginza & Hibiya lines to Ginza, exits A12 & A13** 🕐 **Mon-Sat**

Do it for the Kids

Tokyo can be a wonderful place to pick up toys and games, not least because the Japanese kids' imaginative world is so visually different from the Western one and there is no shortage of creative inventiveness in how that world is represented in toys. From Godzilla to Hello Kitty, something will definitely appeal.

Chris Mellor

Food to Take Home

Tokyo offers incredibly varied choices in food and drink, both Western and Japanese. All the major department stores have massive underground 'food floors' packed with every imaginable delicacy. See also the **Nihonshu Jōhōkan** (p. 35) and the **Tsukiji Shijo External Market** (p. 29) for places to pick up sake and food.

9.30am-7pm, Sun 9.30am-6pm

Muji (6, B5)
Who can resist this no-name designer label, that took Japan then Paris and London by storm. Great inexpensive souvenirs here, from do-it-yourself soy sauce seasonings, to cool, pure white toddler cycles. This is the flagship store but look for branches in Tokyo department stores.
✉ Minato-ku, Kita-Aoyama 2-12-18
☎ 3478 5800
🚇 Ginza line to Gaienmae, exit 2
🕐 10am-8pm

Yoshitoku (3, F9)
Doll-maker to the emperor, this place, next to subway, has been in business since 1711. It's possible to buy a smaller piece for around ¥2000. For the larger ones? The sky's the limit.
✉ Taitō-ku, Asakusabashi 1-9-14
☎ 3863 4419
🚇 Sōbu line to Asakusabashi, exit A2
🕐 9.30am-5.30pm

FOR CHILDREN
Hakuhinkan Toy Park (12, H4) A huge toy shop crammed to the ceiling with models of Doraemon the robotic blue cat, Dragonball, Pikachu and even Japanese nostalgia favourites such as Ultraman, Ultra 7 and Nyarome, the mischievous cat. There's a theatre and a very child-friendly restaurant.
✉ Chūō-ku, Ginza 8-8-11 ☎ 3571 8008
🚇 Toei Asakusa & Ginza lines to Shimbashi, exits 1 & 3
🚃 Yamanote line to Shimbashi, Ginza exit
🕐 11am-8pm

Kiddyland (6, D3)
Five floors of products that your children would probably die for and you may still be paying for next year. The Sanrio products and more specifically her feline highness Hello Kitty are in constant high demand.
✉ Shibuya-ku, Jingūmae 6-1-9
☎ 3409 3431
🚇 Chiyoda line to Meiji-jingūmae, exit 4
🕐 10am-8pm

FOOD & DRINK
National Azabu (3, L5) Posher than posh can be, this is where the ambassadorial lackeys are sent to stock up on pate de foie gras and truffles or their Japanese equivalents, *uni* (sea-urchin) and *mat-sutake* (mushrooms). You should stock up too.
✉ Minato-ku, Minami-Azabu 4-5-2
☎ 3442 3181
🚇 Hibiya line to Hiro-o, exits 1 & 2
🕐 9.30am-7pm

John Ashburne

For goodness – sake

places to eat

Beyond international exports such as sushi, tempura and sukiyaki, there's over twenty different forms of Japanese cooking to sample. Except **shokudō** (all-around eateries; we've described these as 'Japanese') and **izakaya** (drinking restaurants), every restaurant in Japan specialises in one cuisine, so don't expect variety from menus. Rice is, naturally, central to every meal with the word *gohan* used for both 'rice' and 'meal'.

O-ikura Desu Ka?
Prices are for one, without drinks

¥	less than ¥2000
¥¥	¥2000-¥4999
¥¥¥	5000-¥10,000
¥¥¥¥	over ¥10,000

John Ashburne

Eating Tokyo Style

If ever a city was destined for permanent indigestion, it's this one. Tokyoites rarely bother with *asa-gohan* ('morning rice') breakfast. Maybe a quick coffee and a slice of doorstep-thick toast, the *mōningu setto*, 'morning set', ubiquitous at the city's thousands of **kissaten** or coffee shops.

Lunch is an equally hurried affair. Most likely it's a *higawari teishoku*, the special set menus that change daily at the mom-and-pop canteens, **shokudō**, that dot the business districts. A rice dish, miso soup and fried fish is the classic choice. Or else it'll be a bowl of rāmen noodles at a favourite store. Or buckwheat noodles at a **tachigui** noodle stop where customers in a hurry stand up to eat Japan's proto-fast food. Incontrovertible scientific research shows that Tokyoites slurp their noodles, on average, 3mm per second slower than their Osaka counterparts. So they say.

Dinner is the only time city dwellers really get to relax. Usually it's over beer and yakitori (similar to chicken kebab) or **tonkatsu** (breaded pork-cutlets) or tempura, at a neighbourhood izakaya. On special occasions

Drinks

Introduced at the end of the last century, *biiru* (beer) is now the favourite tipple of the Japanese, especially lager. Draught beer, *nama biiru*, is widely available as are imported beers. The production of *sake* (rice wine) was once restricted to imperial brewers but later produced at temples and shrines across the country. It plays an important part in most celebrations and festivals and is served *atsukan* (warm) in winter and *reishu* (cold) in summer. *Shōchū* (used as a disinfectant in the Edo period) is a distilled spirit (30% alcohol) that has been reinvented as the trendy drink, *chūhai* (with soda and lemon). Japanese wine is often blended with imports from South America or Eastern Europe, while French and Italian wine is popular in modern restaurants and cafes. Local whiskey is usually drunk *mizu-wari* (with water and ice) or *onzarokku* (on the rocks).

Espresso *kōhii* (coffee) is easily available in Tokyo thanks to chains of Euro-style cafes like Doutor or Pronto. At a cafe you'll be asked whether you like your coffee *hotto* (hot) or *aisu* (cold). Black tea also comes hot or cold, with *miruku* (milk) or *remon* (lemon). Japanese tea is green and the powdered form used in tea ceremony, *matcha,* is drunk after being whipped into a frothy consistency. More common is leafy green tea, *o-cha,* which is drunk after being steeped in a pot.

they'll opt for **yōshoku** (Western cuisine) or treat themselves to a **kappo** (upmarket izakaya), or sushi. The choices are endless. Yet Tokyoites are creatures of culinary habit. Chances are they'll be regular customers at the same spot – day-in day-out – *jōrenkyaku*.

Cuisines & Restaurants

Ubiquitous shokudō are Japan's most popular restaurants and recognisable by their tacky plastic window displays. The best deals are the lunch and sometimes dinner speciality, *teishoku* (set course). To order quickly, follow the lead of stressed-out salarymen and ask for *kyō-no-ranchi* (today's lunch) to avoid the time-wasting menu.

Looking almost good enough to eat: fantastic plastic food

Izakaya are Japanese pubs with a choice of seating either around the counter, at a table or on the tatami floor. They serve hearty drinking fare, like *yakisoba* (fried noodles with meat and vegetables).

Robatayaki are also drinking restaurants, though the name means 'hearthside cooking' as dishes are grilled by the chef. At an **okonomiyaki**, you do the cooking of meat, seafood and vegetables in an egg batter while sitting around a *teppan* (iron hotplate).

For an after-work treat with drinks grab sushi at a **kaiten-zushi**, where food ambles by on a conveyor belt in front of diners. Many foreigners enjoy sukiyaki and Tokyo's best restaurants use high-quality thinly sliced Kōbe beef, simmered in a broth of soy sauce, sugar and sake, and serve with tofu or vegetables. Like sukiyaki, **shabu-shabu** consists of thinly sliced beef in a light broth, then dipped in tangy sesame seed and citrus sauces.

Borrowed from the Portuguese, **tempura** has become known as uniquely Japanese. For the total experience order teishoku, which includes miso soup and rice. With origins in China, **rāmen**, is a generous bowl of noodles in a meat or fish broth and has become one of the city's most popular fast food options.

A highlight of any Tokyo visit is **unagi** (eel) cooked over hot coals and basted with a rich sake and soy sauce. Budget diners might opt for the *unagi bento* (boxed lunches) as full meals can carry a hefty price tag. The gourmet pinnacle of Tokyo is **kaiseki**, a fusion of ingredients, preparation, setting and presentation based on the tea ceremony. Meals are served in small courses so you can admire the craft in each dish and is ideally experienced in a private room of a **ryōtei** (traditional restaurant) overlooking a tranquil Japanese garden.

AKASAKA, NAGATA-CHŌ & TORANOMON

Chez Prisi (8, D3) ¥¥
Swiss
This is the place to head
for when you're 'tofu-ed
out', and need a calorie-
laden fondue fix. Daily
lunch specials are adver-
tised on a blackboard in
the window. It's just past
the police box; look for the
English sign.
✉ Minato-ku, Akasaka
2-12-33, Akasaka Ebisu
Bldg, B1F ☎ 3224
9877 Ⓜ Ginza &
Namboku lines to
Tameike-sannō, exit 11
🕐 Mon-Sat 11.30am-
10pm

Fisherman's Wharf
(8, B2) ¥¥¥
American
You keep expecting
Captain Ahab to walk in
the door, but the crab,

shrimp and oysters, pre-
pared American-style, are
undeniably good.
✉ Minato-ku, Akasaka
3-17-8, Dobashi Bldg,
B1F ☎ 3583 0659
Ⓜ Ginza & Marunouchi
lines to Akasaka-
mitsuke, east exit
🕐 Mon-Sat 11am-
11pm ♿

Keyaki Grill
(8, C3) ¥¥¥
Continental European
Despite its name, this is
not your local greasy
spoon, but rather Tokyo's
most highly praised practi-
tioner in its field.
✉ Chiyoda-ku, Nagata-
chō 2-10-3, Capitol
Tōkyū Hotel, B1F
☎ 3581 8514
Ⓜ Ginza & Namboku
lines to Tameike-sannō,

exit 5 🕐 noon-3pm,
5.30-10pm

Mugyodon (8, D3) ¥¥
Korean
This is a very popular and
extremely friendly place. It's
also a rare chance to sample the real Korean McCoy
in Tokyo, not the adulter-
ated Japanese version.
✉ Minato-ku, Akasaka
2-17-74, Akasaka
Sangyo Bldg, 2F
☎ 3586 6478
Ⓜ Ginza & Namboku
lines to Tameike-sannō,
exit 11 🕐 Mon-Sat
5pm-midnight

Sushi-sei (8, C2) ¥¥
Sushi
You'll find top-notch sushi
and a great sushi-bar
atmosphere at Sushi-sei.
Everyone sits at counters
observing chefs in constant
motion. The *jō-nigiri* is
good value. Look for the
noren (curtains) in the
doorway and at peak times
expect to queue.
✉ Minato-ku, Akasaka
3-11-4, Bergo Akasaka, 1F
☎ 3582 9503
Ⓜ Ginza & Marunouchi
lines to Akasaka-
mitsuke, west exit
🕐 Mon-Sat 11.30am-
2pm, 5-10.30pm

Tōfuya (8, C3) ¥¥
Tofu
The authentic tofu specialist
that also offers grilled fish
and rice dishes. Lunch is
great value here: there are
usually four sets to choose
from. It's a little tricky to
find as it's on a small side
street, a street west of
Sotobori-dōri. Look for a
traditional exterior across
from an electronics shop.
✉ Minato-ku, Akasaka

*Japan's most famous export: sushi. Experience the real
thing in Tokyo, be amazed at the possible variations.*

The Taste of Old Tokyo

Missing out on a 'real' Japanese experience? Sit down for a meal in a traditional Japanese restaurant. The following are a few select old Tokyo restaurants that are well worth seeking out:

Botan – funky chicken, Kanda (p. 74)
Chichibu Nishiki – rustic 'n' rough for Ginza (p. 78)
Echikatsu – smart sukiyaki, Ueno (p. 86)
Inakaya – glad to be trad, Roppongi (p. 83)
Kanda Yabu Soba – cool noodles, Kanda (p. 74)
Komagata Dojō – loach no less, Asakusa (p. 75)
Matsuya – buckwheat bliss, Kanda (p. 74)
Tonton Honten – fast tasty snacks under-the-tracks, Yūrakuchō (p. 80)

3-5-2, Sanyo Akasaka Bldg, 1F ☎ 3582 1028
🚇 Ginza & Namboku lines to Tameike-sannō, exit 10
🕐 Mon-Fri 11.30am-1.30pm, 5-11pm ♿ V

Tohkalin (8, E5) ¥¥¥¥
Chinese
Arch-rival to Aux Sept Bonheurs, Tohkalin claims to have the best Chinese food in Tokyo. It's a close call, but Tokhalin holds one unbeatable trump card – it has access to Hotel Ōkura's indomitable wine cellar.
✉ Minato-ku, Toranomon 2-10-4, Hotel Ōkura, 6F
☎ 3505 6068
🚇 Ginza & Hibiya lines to Toranomon, exit 2
🕐 11.30am-2.30pm, 5.30-9.30pm

Tokyo Joe's (8, B3) ¥¥¥
American
Fortunately Tokyo Joe's doesn't overdo the nautical theme. The speciality here is stone crab, imported daily from Florida. It's tasty stuff, but wouldn't you prefer homegrown cuisine? Comfort food for homesick statesiders.
✉ Chiyoda-ku, Nagatachō 2-13-5, Akasaka Eight-One Bldg, B1F
☎ 3508 0325
🚇 Ginza & Marunouchi lines to Akasaka-mitsuke, east exit
🕐 11.30am-3pm, 5-11pm ♿

Trattoria Marumo (8, B2) ¥¥
Italian
Italian food is really popular in Tokyo and this is a pleasant, atmospheric pizzeria that's easy to find – look for the display case full of plastic pizzas in the windows. There's a more formal Marumo on Akasaka-dōri.
✉ Minato-ku, Akasaka 3-8-14, Tōyama Bldg, 1F ☎ 3585 5371
🚇 Ginza & Marunouchi lines to Akasaka-mitsuke, west exit
🕐 11.30am-midnight ♿

EBISU & DAIKANYAMA

Ippu-dō (7, B5) ¥
Rāmen
Another nationally famous rāmen shop, specialising in tonkatsu pork-broth noodles. The *akamaru shinmi rāmen* is tailored towards the Tokyo palate, the *shiromaru* is pure Kyūshū. Nice decor, friendly staff, and, er, 1950s US surf tunes. It's just east of Shibuya-bashi post office. Expect to queue.
✉ Shibuya-ku, Hiro-o 1-3-13, Haines Bldg, 1F
☎ 5420 2225
🚇 Hibiya line to Ebisu, exits 1 & 2
🕐 11am-4pm ♿

Shunsenbō (7, A4) ¥¥
Shabu-shabu
You'll find great value for money at this restaurant specialising in tofu dishes and shabu-shabu. Recommended for vegetarians – the tofu that is. There's also an English menu.
✉ Shibuya-ku, Hiro-o 1-1-40, Ebisu Prime Square Plaza, 1F
☎ 5469 9761
🚇 Hibiya line to Ebisu, exits 1 & 2
🕐 11am-3pm, 5.30-11pm

Taillevent-Robuchon (7, D5) ¥¥¥
French
Top-notch fare for lovers of all things French in this faithful reproduction of a Louis XV chateau. It's very posh and can be found in the grounds of the Ebisu Garden Place complex.
✉ Meguro-ku, Sanda 1-13-1, Ebisu Garden Place
☎ 5424 1338
🚆 Yamanote line to Ebisu, Ebisu Garden Place exit 🕐 noon-2pm, 6-9.30pm

AKIHABARA & KANDA

Botan (13, C8)   ¥¥¥
Japanese
Traditional restaurant serving *torisuki,* an Edo-period pot-stew. Guaranteed to be a culinary highlight of a visit to Tokyo. Reservations are recommended.
✉ Chiyoda-ku, Kanda Sudachō 1-15
☎ 3251 0577
Ⓖ Ginza line to Suda, exit 6
🕐 Mon-Sat 11.30am-9pm

Jangara Rāmen Honten (13, A8)   ¥
Rāmen
You'll have to queue to get a table here, but its worth it. The original shop in a hugely popular chain, specialising in Kyūshū-style noodles in that notoriously stinky pork broth. The *zenbuiri rāmen* has a bit of everything in it. Branches in Akasaka and Harajuku.
✉ Chiyoda-ku, Soto-Kanda 3-11-6
☎ 3251 4059
Ⓖ Ginza line to Suehirochō, exit 3
🕐 Mon-Sat 10.30am-11.30pm

Kanda Yabu Soba (13, C8)   ¥¥
Soba
Soba mecca for the buckwheat noodle aficionados of Tokyo. A Kanda institution, its authentic surroundings add to the atmosphere. Yet it's the noodles that make the day. Look for queues of excited customers in front of a traditional Japanese building in a traditional garden setting, surrounded by a wooden fence.
✉ Chiyoda-ku, Kanda

Rāmen – Tokyo's traditonal fast food

Awajichō 2-10
☎ 3251 0287
Ⓖ Toei Shinjuku line to Ogawamachi, exit A3
🕐 11.30am-8pm ♿

Matsuya (13, C8)   ¥¥
Soba
Rival to Yabu Soba and located almost next door, Matsuya is less crowded, though still hugely popular. Try plain *zaru* soba, then follow it up with the *kamo nanban,* soba with slices of roast duck. The waitresses here are friendly-but-tough dames of the old Edo school.
✉ Chiyoda-ku, Kanda Sudachō 1-13
☎ 3251 1556
Ⓖ Toei Shinjuku line to Ogawamachi, exit A3
🕐 Mon-Sat 11am-8pm ♿

Muito Bom (3, G7)   ¥¥
Brazilian
Plenty of good value fare at this tiny place located in the very heart of Kanda's bookstore-riddled Jimbōchō. The Mequeca fish stew, a speciality of Bahia, is especially recommended. The restaurant is upstairs from Muang Thai Nabe restaurant, behind the Iwanami Hall.
✉ Chiyoda-ku, Kanda Jimbōchō 2-1, Iwanami Jimbōchō Bldg, Annex 2F
☎ 3238 7946
Ⓖ Hanzōmon, Toei Mita & Toei Shinjuku lines to Jimbōchō, exit A6
🕐 Mon-Sat 5.30-10.30pm

ASAKUSA

Edokko
(11, B2) ¥¥
Tempura
Famed restaurant serving that great Asakusa speciality, tempura, in a very authentic atmosphere. Try its *tendon*, shrimp tempura on rice as a treat for lunch. The restaurant has a traditional wooden facade and a white *noren* curtain outside.
✉ Taitō-ku, Asakusa 1-40-7 ☎ 3841 0150 Ⓖ Ginza & Toei Asakusa lines to Asakusa, exit 6 ⏱ Wed-Mon 11.30am-9pm ⚲

Komagata Dojō
(11, E3) ¥¥
Japanese
This is an elegant old Shitamachi restaurant that specialises in *dojō* (loach, similar to an eel), and it comes highly recommended. It's in a very traditional-looking building next to a small park, near the Sumidagawa river.
✉ Taitō-ku, Komagata 1-7-12 ☎ 3842 4001 Ⓖ Ginza & Toei Asakusa lines to Asakusa, exit A1 ⏱ 11am-9pm ⚲

La Ranarata
(11, D5) ¥¥¥
Italian
Good Milanese cuisine on the 22nd floor of the Asahi Beer building affords vertigo. Enjoy sigh-inducing views across Asakusa and the Sumida-gawa river and even better pizza capricciosa.
✉ Sumida-ku, Azumabashi 1-23-1, Asahi Beer Azumabashi Bldg, Asahi Beer Tower 22F ☎ 5608 5277 Ⓖ Toei Asakusa line to Honjo-Azumabashi, main exit; Ginza & Toei Asakusa lines to Asakusa, exit 1 ⏱ 11.30am-2pm, 4.30-9pm

Owariya (11, C2) ¥
Tempura
This popular place on Kaminarimon-dōri serves tempura and a variety of noodle dishes. The *tempura donburi* comes especially recommended. Gets crowded at lunch.
✉ Taitō-ku, Asakusa 1-7-1 ☎ 3845 4500 Ⓖ Ginza & Toei Asakusa lines to Asakusa, exit 1 ⏱ Sat-Thurs 11.30am-8.30pm ⚲

Raishūken
(11, B1) ¥
Rāmen
Blissfully good rāmen. Take a step back in time when you enter this 40 year-old noodle shop. The locals describe this as *'natsukashii aji'* or 'the taste of nostalgia'. Order an *ōmori* – large bowl of Taiwan-style wavy noodles in a soy-based broth. Unmissable.
✉ Taitō-ku, Nishi-Asakusa 2-26-3 ☎ 3844 7409 Ⓖ Ginza & Toei Asakusa lines to Asakusa, exit 6 ⏱ Wed-Mon, noon-7pm ⚲

Tonkyū (11, C4) ¥
Tonkatsu
Cosy family-run restaurant where the specialty is good tonkatsu at reasonable prices. Its *rōsu katsu teishoku* lunch is excellent. It is just to the right of Kaminari-mon Gate.
✉ Taitō-ku, Asakusa 1-2-6 ☎ 3841 8718 Ⓖ Ginza & Toei Asakusa lines to Asakusa, exit 1 ⏱ Fri-Wed 10am-8pm ⚲

John McInnes

Great Views
Skyscraper dining is one of Tokyo's more memorable experiences. The luxury hotels in west Shinjuku provide the prime hunting ground for high-altitude haute cuisine. Try the **New York Grill** on the 52nd floor of the Park Hyatt (p. 101), or head over to Asakusa and **La Ranarata** (see above) atop the Asahi Beer Building. Or for a more humble repast in the clouds, take a rice ball to the observation deck of the **Tokyo Metropolitan Government Offices** (p. 41), pictured left, 202m above west Shinjuku.

AOYAMA, HARAJUKU & OMOTE-SANDŌ

Aux Sept Bonheurs
(6, D4) ¥¥¥
Chinese
Boutique Chinese cuisine served in the style of a fine French restaurant. This is justly one of Tokyo's most highly regarded restaurants. The courses are a fabulous succession of small but wonderfully prepared delicacies.
✉ Minato-ku, Kita-Aoyama 3-6-1, Hanae Mori Bldg, 5F
☎ 3498 8144
🚇 Chiyoda, Ginza & Hanzōmon lines to Omote-sandō, exit A1
🕙 11.30am-3pm, 5-11pm

Fonda de la Madrugada
(6, A2) ¥¥¥
Mexican
Tokyo's best Mexican cuisine can be found at Fonda. This favourite with expats and the business community is up past the Turkish embassy in Jingūmae. For authentic atmosphere it comes complete with an open courtyard and strolling musicians – everything from the roof tiles to the chefs has been imported from Mexico. Hope you like mariachi though.
✉ Shibuya-ku, Jingūmae 2-33-12, Villa Bianca B1F

Fusion and friends at Fujimama's

☎ 5410 6288
🚉 Yamanote line to Harajuku, Takeshita exit 🕙 Mon-Thurs 5.30pm-2am, Fri-Sat 5.30pm-5am

Fujimama's
(6, D2) ¥¥
Fusion
Very pleasant, hugely popular fusion restaurant, presided over by chef/co-owner Mark Vann. Good California wines are available and there are nice tatami rooms upstairs in what was once a tatami-maker's place. It's directly behind the Penny Black store. Reservations are recommended.
✉ Shibuya-ku, Jingūmae 6-3-2
☎ 5485 2262
🚇 Chiyoda line to Meiji-Jingūmae, exit 4
🕙 11am-10pm [V]

Home (6, D4) ¥¥
Vegetarian
A veritable vegetarian oasis in the meat munching capital. The organic lunch is excellent and good value. Hiroba, its sister store, offers similar take-out fare. Both are in Crayon House building just off Omote-sandō, one block behind the Hanae Mori complex.
✉ Minato-ku, Kita-Aoyama 3-8-15 Crayon House B1F
☎ 3406 6409
🚇 Chiyoda, Ginza & Hanzōmon lines to Omote-sandō, exits B2 & B4
🕙 11am-10pm 🔆 [V]

L'Amphore
(6, C4) ¥¥¥¥
French
One of the best French restaurants in the city – the atmosphere is spot-on and

Vegetarians
In the late 1800s, the centuries-old Buddhist prohibition against eating meat was repealed. It's been downhill for Japanese vegetarians ever since. Seek out one of the handful of organic restaurants, a tofu specialist, or stick to the tofu, bean and vegetable dishes in an *izakaya*. Look for the [V] with each review. Be warned – Tokyo is a carnivorous city.

it avoids the overly formal feeling which is the bane of so many top-end French places in Tokyo. It's easy to spot; look for the French sign outside.
✉ Shibuya-ku, Jingūmae 3-5-4
☎ 3402 6486
🚇 Ginza & Hanzōmon lines to Gaienmae, exit 2
🕑 Thurs-Tues 11.30am-2pm, 5.30-9.30pm

Las Chicas (6, E3) ¥¥
Brasserie
Pleasant, spacious joint where cool and wannabe-cool expats come to pose and peer. Everything from lattes to fine dining, either out on the terrace or beside the fireplace – and the wine list is solid. Las Chicas is housed in a former embassy run by the arts umbrella organisation Vision Network. Nude Lounge upstairs is less formal.
✉ Shibuya-ku, Jingūmae 5-47-6
☎ 3407 6865
🚇 Chiyoda, Ginza & Hanzōmon lines to Omote-sandō, exit B2
🕑 11am-11pm V

L'Orangerie de Paris (6, D4) ¥¥¥
French
In the Hanae Mori building on Omote-sandō, this is an elegant choice for lovers of French cuisine. The lunch set is good value and dinners are reliable. Especially recommended is the Sunday brunch.
✉ Minato-ku, Kita-Aoyama 3-10-13
☎ 3407 7461
🚇 Chiyoda, Ginza & Hanzōmon lines to Omote-sandō, exit B2
🕑 Mon-Sat 11.30am-3.30pm, 5.30-9.30pm, Sun 11am-3.30pm

Tea Ceremony

It takes years to master yet seems so simple to the novice. The Japanese tea ceremony, *chanoyu*, combines the art and aesthetics of cooking, ceramics, haiku, calligraphy and flower arrangement. It's the perfect respite from frenetic Tokyo. In terms of your taste buds, be prepared for the bitter yet creamy green tea followed by super-sweet red bean cakes.

The following hotels offer tea ceremonies to visitors along with explanations in English: **Imperial Hotel** (☎ 3504 1111; Mon-Sat 10am-4pm; ¥1500), **Hotel Ōkura** (☎ 3582 0111; 11am-noon, 1-5pm; ¥1050) and **Hotel New Ōtani** (☎ 3265 1111; Thurs-Sat, 11am & 1pm; ¥1050).

Oliver Strewe

Monsoon Cafe (3, K4) ¥¥
Brasserie
Decent pan-Asian fare in this very popular semi-outdoor restaurant. Most customers come to see and be seen. It's a fun spot for tropical drinks and just hanging out, though there's an annoying 2-hr limit at busy times. Also branches in Shibuya and Daikanyama.
✉ Minato-ku, Minami-Aoyama 7-3-1
☎ 3400 7200
🚇 Hibiya line to Hiro-o, exit 3 🕑 11.30-5am

Tony Roma's (6, B5) ¥¥
American
Calorie-crazy American-style ribs and onion rings, and salads for the not so hungry. Occasional additions of seafood to the menu – just for something different. There's also a popular branch in Roppongi.
✉ Minato-ku, Minami-Aoyama 3-1-30, Sumitomo Bldg, B1F
☎ 3479 5214
🚇 Ginza line to Gaienmae, exit 1
🕑 noon-11pm ♿

GINZA, NIHONBASHI, TSUKIJI & YŪRAKUCHŌ

Buono Buono
(12, G4)   ¥¥
Italian
Doubly *buono* indeed. This place offers good value, above-average Italian fare on the 2nd floor of Nishi Ginza department store, in front of the Mullion building.
✉ Chūō-ku, Ginza 4-1-2, Nishi Ginza department store 2F
☎ 3566 4031
Ⓜ Ginza, Marunouchi & Hibiya lines to Ginza, exit C6
🕐 11.30am-11pm ☂

Chichibu Nishiki
(12, F5)   ¥¥
Izakaya
Atmospheric and traditional, this *nomiya* has tasty, inexpensive food in a very authentic setting. It's tucked away behind the Kabuki-za theatre, north of the Ginza Dai-Ichi Hotel.
✉ Chūō-ku, Ginza 2-13-14 ☎ 3541 4777
Ⓜ Toei Asakusa & Hibiya lines to Higashi-Ginza, exit A7
🕐 Mon-Fri 5-10.30pm

Edogin Sushi
(12, H6)   ¥¥¥
Sushi
Justly famous for its fresh, oversized, but reasonably priced Edo-style sushi. At dinnertime it's worth paying a little extra to get the *toku-jōnigiri* sushi set. There is no English sign outside, but it's easily identified by the plastic sushi in the window.
✉ Chūō-ku, Tsukiji 4-5-1
☎ 3543 4401
Ⓜ Hibiya & Toei Asakusa lines to Higashi-Ginza, exit 6
🕐 11am-9pm

Funachū (12, G4)   ¥¥
Izakaya
Slightly upmarket izakaya towards Yūrakuchō. Try the mini-kaiseki set meal. The classic yakitori goes well with the ice-cold beer – a great pick-me-up after a hard day's shopping on the streets of Ginza.
✉ Chūō-ku, Ginza 6-108, Coridōgai 2F
☎ 3572 0712
Ⓜ Ginza line to Ginza,

exit A3 🕐 Mon-Fri 11.30am-2pm, 5pm-midnight, Sat-Sun 11.30am-9pm

Kyubei (12, H4)   ¥¥¥¥
Sushi
Ginza power-sushi dining at its most elegant. It's not just sushi you're paying for, it's the wonderful surroundings. Discreet to the point of being almost unfindable, so look for the very elegant Japanese facade set back from the street.
✉ Chūō-ku, Ginza 8-7-6
☎ 3571 6523
Ⓜ Ginza line to Shimbashi, exit 2
🕐 Mon-Sat 11.30am-2pm, 5-10pm

Maxim's de Paris
(12, G4)   ¥¥¥¥
French
Ever seen a Japanese waiter attempt a Gallic shrug? Superior French cuisine is graciously served in this basement restaurant. The interior and the menu are dead ringers for the original in Paris.
✉ Chūō-ku, Ginza 5-3-1, Sony Bldg, B3F
☎ 3572 3621
Ⓜ Ginza, Hibiya & Marunouchi lines to Ginza, exit B9
🕐 Mon-Sat 11.30am-11pm

Munakata
(12, J4)   ¥¥¥
Kaiseki
Good value kaiseki sets are the highlight of this place.
✉ Chūō-ku, Ginza 8-6-15, Mitsui Urban Hotel B1F
☎ 3574 9356 Ⓜ Ginza line to Shimbashi, exit 3
🕐 7-9am, 11.30am-3pm, 5-10pm

Under the tracks in Yurakūchō's Yakitori Alley

Oliver Strewe

Muromachi Sunaba
(12, B4)   ¥¥

Soba

Third in the soba triumvirate, the 'Sand Pit' is less cocky than Kanda Yabu Soba and even more laid back than Matsuya. Try the excellent *tenzaru* soba with a side order of yakitori. There's also a branch of Akasaka.

✉ **Chūō-ku, Nihonbashi Muromachi 4-1-13**
☎ **3241 4038**
🚇 **Sōbu line to Shin-Nihonbashi, exit 4**
🕐 **Mon-Sat 11am-8pm** ♿

Soba noodles in the 'Sand Pit' – Muromachi Sunaba

Nair's (12, G6)   ¥¥

Indian

Oft-praised in the Japanese media, Nair's small scale allows proper attention to be paid to the food. Reservations are recommended and with luck you'll get a table next to one of the latest teenage pop idols.

✉ **Chūō-ku, Ginza 4-10-7**
☎ **3541 8246**
🚇 **Hibiya & Toei Asakusa lines to Higashi-Ginza, exit 1**
🕐 **11am-9pm**

New Torigin
(12, G5)   ¥¥

Yakitori

It's really not so new, but who cares. Good sake for sampling and even better yakitori at this unpretentious popular place, tucked away down a back alley in the heart of Ginza. Signage and menu in English.

✉ **Chūō-ku, Ginza 5-5-11** ☎ **3571 3334**
🚇 **Ginza, Hibiya & Marunouchi lines to Ginza, exit C2**
🕐 **Mon-Fri 4am-10pm, Sat-Sun 11.30am-9.30pm**

Robata (12, G4)   ¥¥

Izakaya

Tokyo's most celebrated izakaya and a place where, if you don't speak Japanese, you're going to have to bring a friend who does; point at what your neighbour is eating; or throw yourself at the mercy of the staff and say *'omakase shimasu'* ('you decide').

✉ **Chiyoda-ku, Yūrakuchō 1-3-8**
☎ **3591 1905**
🚇 **Hibiya & Chiyoda lines to Hibiya, exit A4**
🕐 **5am-11pm**

Sabatine di Firenze
(12, G4)   ¥¥¥¥

Italian

In the same building as Maxim's de Paris, this restaurant serves excellent northern Italian fare in a faithful reproduction of its twin in Florence. Everything is over-the-top Italian, but the prices are reasonable considering the location.

✉ **Chūō-ku, Ginza 5-3-1, Sony Bldg, 7F**
☎ **3573 0013**
🚇 **Ginza, Hibiya & Marunouchi lines to Ginza, exit B9**
🕐 **noon-3pm, 5.30-11pm**

Shin-hi-no-moto
(12, F3)   ¥¥

Izakaya

It's the travelling gourmet's dream come true – an izakaya in Tokyo run by a native English speaker. This is a lively spot under the train tracks in Yūrakuchō. A great chance to enjoy the izakaya experience without language hassles. It's located opposite JAL Plaza.

✉ **Chiyoda-ku, Yūrakuchō 2-4-4**
☎ **3214 8021**
🚇 **Ginza, Hibiya & Marunouchi lines to Ginza, exit A0**
🕐 **5pm-midnight**

Ten-Ichi
(12, G4)   ¥¥¥¥

Tempura

One of Tokyo's oldest and best tempura restaurants, this is the place to try tempura the way it's meant to be: light and crispy, not as soggy as an old hand-towel. There are also branches in the Imperial Hotel, the basement of the Sony Building and in Akasaka, but the Ginza restaurant is the smartest and the best.

✉ **Chūō-ku, Ginza 6-6-5**
☎ **3571 1949**
🚇 **Ginza & Hibiya lines to Ginza, exit B7**
🕐 **11.30am-9.30pm** ♿

Oodles of Noodles

Soba noodles are thin, brown, buckwheat noodles, while *udon* noodles are thick, white, wheat noodles. Most Japanese noodle shops serve both soba and udon prepared in a variety of ways. Noodles are usually served in a bowl containing a light, bonito-flavoured broth, but you can also order them served cold and piled on a bamboo screen with a cold broth for dipping.

By far the most popular type of cold noodles is *zaru soba*, which is served with bits of *nori* (seaweed) on top. This comes with a small plate of *wasabi* and sliced scallions – put these into the cup of broth and eat the noodles by dipping them in this mixture. At the end of your meal, the waiter will give you some hot broth to mix with the leftover sauce, which you drink like a kind of tea. As with *rāmen*, feel free to slurp as loudly as you please.

Oliver Strewe

Tonton Honten

(12, G3)　　　¥¥
Izakaya
Not for the hard-of-hearing. Another friendly, noisy, informal place at Yūrakuchō. Clutch your beer and their speciality, yakitori, as the bullet trains roar overhead every few minutes. It's in the east-west tunnel and even boasts an English menu.
✉ Chiyoda-ku, Yūrakuchō 2-1-10
☎ 3508 9454
🚇 Ginza, Hibiya & Marunouchi lines to Ginza, exit C2
🕐 3-11.30pm ⚇

Tsukiji Sushikō

(12, G6)　　　¥
Sushi
Excellent value, super clean and spacious sushi place, on the corner next to the Kyōbashi post office. The decor is tastefully elegant and its location, just a raw octopus' throw from Tsukiji Shijo market, means the sushi's always fresh. Also a branch in Roppongi.
✉ Chuō-ku, Tsukiji 4-7-1
☎ 3547 0505
🚇 Hibiya line to Tsukiji, exits 1 & 2 🕐 Mon-Fri 11am-3pm, 5-11pm, Sat-Sun 11am-11pm ⚇ [V]

IKEBUKURO

Akiyoshi (2, B1)　¥¥
Yakitori
There's plenty of tasty yakitori to be had in this noisy unpretentious establishment. Watch out for the spicy mustard dipping sauce though – it's hotter than you think. There's no English signage outside, but you can easily spot the long counters and flaming grills from the street. The large picture menu is also helpful for non-Japanese speakers. There are also branches of Akiyoshi across the city.
✉ Toshima-ku, Nishi-Ikebukuro 3-30-4, KH Bldg, 1F
☎ 3982 0644
🚇 Marunouchi & Yūrakuchō lines to Ikebukuro, exit 1a
🚃 Yamanote line to Ikebukuro, west exit
🕐 5-11pm

Chez Kibeau
(2, B1)　　　¥¥¥
European
Fine continental cuisine in a pleasant, relaxing basement. Let English-speaking owner Kibo-san make all the difficult gastronomic decisions and enjoy the wine. Far more civilised than the madness at street level.
✉ Toshima-ku, Nishi-Ikebukuro 3-22-7

☎ 3987 6666
Ⓜ Marunouchi & Yūrakuchō lines to Ikebukuro, exits 1a & 1b
◷ Tues-Sun, 6pm-midnight

Komazushi (2, C4)   ¥
Sushi
Revolving but not revolting sushi restaurant that is handily located on the east side of Ikebukuro station. It's popular and friendly, and near a giant *pachinko* parlour.
✉ Toshima-ku, Higashi-Ikebukuro 1-11-1, Hotel Whitecity, 1F ☎ 3590 0581
Ⓜ Marunouchi &

Yūrakuchō lines to Ikebukuro, exit 35
🚉 Yamanote line to Ikebukuro, east exit
◷ 11am-10pm ⚥

Sasashu (2, B1)   ¥¥¥
Izakaya
Sasashu is a high quality sake specialist and serves *kamonabe* (duck stew). A little Japanese language ability would come in handy here. Across the street from a liquor store, its dignified old Japanese facade stands out from the strip joints.
✉ Toshima-ku, Ikebukuro 2-2-2
☎ 3971 9363

Ⓜ Marunouchi & Yūrakuchō lines to Ikebukuro, exit 3
◷ Mon-Sat 5-10pm

Tonerian (2, A2)   ¥¥
Izakaya
One of many izakaya in Ikebukuro, Tonerian is a busy place with friendly staff who are used to the occasional gaijin calling in for cold draft beer and assorted tasty morsels.
✉ Toshima-ku, Nishi-Ikebukuro 1-38-9
☎ 3985 0254
Ⓜ Marunouchi & Yūrakuchō lines to Ikebukuro, exit 12
◷ 4-11pm

ŌDAIBA

Khazana (3, N8)   ¥
Indian
Pig out on the all-you-can-eat lunch or munch on a *bhajee* while watching the sunset over the Rainbow Bridge. This a fairly casual spot atop the Deck's Tokyo Beach complex. Try to score one of the coveted tables out on the viewing platform for maximum dining pleasure.
✉ Minato-ku, Daiba 1-6-1, Deck's Tokyo Beach, 5F
☎ 3599 6551
Ⓜ Yurikamome line to Ōdaiba Kaihin-kōen, main exit
◷ 11am-11pm ⚥

Soup Stock Tokyo (3, O9)   ¥
Cafe
'Soup for all!' proclaims this friendly, inexpensive fast soup restaurant. It's located in the bizarre Venus Fort shopping complex and is a hip lunch spot. The adventurous should try the garlic soup with *onsen tamago* (hot-spring boiled eggs) for something different.
✉ Kōtō-ku, Aomi 1-chōme, Palette Town, 3F
☎ 3599 2333
Ⓜ Yurikamome line to Aomi, main exit
◷ 11am-11pm ⚥

Wakō (3, N8)   ¥
Teishoku
You won't find anything too wacky at this standard-fare teishoku place and it's quite easy to find within the Deck's Tokyo Beach shopping complex. Highly recommended is the rather good tonkatsu set – filling and perfect for a break during retail therapy.
✉ Minato-ku, Daiba 1-6-1, Deck's Tokyo Beach, 5F
☎ 3599 6555
Ⓜ Yurikamome line to Ōdaiba Kaihin-kōen, main exit
◷ 11am-11pm ⚥

Oliver Strewe

Noodling Negotiations
Doing business over lunch is not a Japanese custom. Slurping noodles together is. If you want to impress a business partner, suggest you eat at one of the 'big three' famous buckwheat noodle restaurants – **Kanda Yabu Soba** (p. 74), **Matsuya** (p. 74) or **Muromachi Sunaba** (p. 79).

ROPPONGI & NISHI-AZABU

Bellini's Trattoria
(9, C4)   ¥¥
Italian
The espresso coffee hits
the spot, the pizza's just
right and the staff are
friendly at this classic
Italian eatery. It's perfect
for lunch and affords an
excellent opportunity to
take in the local scene
passing by. Look out for
branches across the city.
✉ **Minato-ku, Roppongi
3-14-12, Shūwa
Roppongi Bldg, 1F**
☎ **3470 5650**
🚇 **Hibiya line to
Roppongi, exit 3**
🕐 **11.30am-3pm, 6pm-
4am** ♿ **V**

Bengawan Solo
(9, C2)   ¥¥
Indonesian
Cosy, good value, Indonesian joint on Roppongi-dōri.
The *gado gado* lunch, beef
in coconut cream, and
rijstaffel (smorgasbord) are
favourites. Decor has the
feel of a Kuta Beach sou-
venir shop, though.
✉ **Minato-ku,
Roppongi 7-18-13,
Kaneko Bldg, 1F**

☎ **3408 5698**
🚇 **Hibiya line to
Roppongi, exit 2**
🕐 **Mon-Sat 11.30am-
2.30pm, 5-9.30pm** ♿

Bernd's Bar (9, C5) ¥¥
German
More of a German izakaya
in fact with good food to
accompany the *bier*. The
menus are in German,
Japanese and English –
languages that the owner
speaks with pizzazz.
✉ **Minato-ku,
Roppongi 5-18-1, Pure
Roppongi, 2F**
☎ **5563 9232**
🚇 **Hibiya line to
Roppongi, exit 3**
🕐 **Mon-Sat 5pm-
early am**

Cerveza (9, C4)   ¥¥
International
Around 100 kinds of beer
on offer here and not just
cervezas but a range of
international suds. The
food, from Japanese to
American by way of Asia, is
actually rather good.
✉ **Minato-ku,
Roppongi 3-11-10, Coco
Roppongi Bldg, B1F**

☎ **3478 0077**
🚇 **Hibiya line to
Roppongi, exit 3**
🕐 **Mon-Sat 6pm-
midnight**

Fukuzushi
(9, C4)   ¥¥¥¥
Sushi
Care for a gin fizz with
that raw tuna? Decidedly
more relaxed than some
places in Ginza and
Tsukiji, Fukuzushi has
some of the best sushi in
town. And there's even a
cocktail bar.
✉ **Minato-ku,
Roppongi 5-7-8**
☎ **3402 4116**
🚇 **Hibiya line to
Roppongi, exit 3**
🕐 **Mon-Sat 11.30am-
1.30pm, 5.30-10pm**

Gokoku (9, B2)   ¥¥¥
Japanese, Regional
Popular place that
specialises in the uniquely
Tokyo regional cuisine,
Edo-ryōri. Expect strong,
salty broths, and straight-
forward, tasty fare. The
menu changes daily.
✉ **Minato-ku,
Roppongi 7-4-5,
Inagaki Bldg, B1F**
☎ **3796 3356**
**Hibiya line to
Roppongi, exit 2**
🕐 **Mon-Sat 6pm-
midnight**

Havana Cafe (9, B3) ¥
Cafe
A favourite chill-out spot
prior to a night on the
Roppongi tiles. In addition to
great happy-hour drink spe-
cials, it serves reliable stuff
like burritos and sandwiches.
✉ **Minato-ku,
Roppongi 4-12-2**
☎ **3423 3500**
🚇 **Hibiya line to**

Eating Etiquette
When eating in public in Japan there are some important rules, but they're fairly easy to remember.
Among the more important eating 'rules' are those
regarding chopsticks. Don't stick them upright in your
rice – that's how rice is offered to the dead! Passing
food from your chopsticks to someone else's is a
similar no-no. When taking food from shared plates,
avoid using the business end of your chopsticks –
invert them before reaching for that tasty morsel.
    Before digging in, it's polite to say *'Itadakimasu'*,
literally 'I will receive'. At the end of the meal you
should say *'Gochisō-sama deshita'*, a respectful way
of saying that the meal was good.

Roppongi, exit 4a
🕐 noon-4pm

Inakaya (9, B3)   ¥¥¥¥
Kappo
Inakaya has achieved fame and favour as a top-end kappo restaurant or upmarket robatayaki. It does raucous, bustling, 'don't stand on ceremony' Japanese dining with gusto. There is also a sister restaurant of the same name in Akasaka.
✉ Minato-ku, Roppongi 7-8-4, Yachiyo Bldg
☎ 3405 9866
🚇 Hibiya line to Roppongi, exit 4a
🕐 5pm-5am

Kisso (9, C5)   ¥¥¥
Kaiseki
Tasteful decor matches the tasty kaiseki dishes at this oasis of civilisation in Roppongi. Kisso also sells the elegant tableware that it uses to present its meals. It is in the basement of the trendy, design-mad Axis Building.
✉ Minato-ku, Roppongi 5-17-1, Axis Bldg, B1F ☎ 3582 4191 🚇 Hibiya line to

Kaiten-zushi – *where dishes rotate on a conveyor belt.*

Roppongi, exit 3
🕐 Mon-Sat 11am-2pm, 5.30-10pm ♿

Moti Darbar
(9, C4)   ¥¥
Indian
A justifiably popular Indian restaurant serving up some of Tokyo's best Indian food. The restaurant has a pleasant atmosphere and the service is very attentive. There are also branches in Akasaka.
✉ Minato-ku, Roppongi 6-2-35, Hama Bldg, 3F
☎ 3479 1939
🚇 Hibiya line to Roppongi, exit 1
🕐 11.30am-11pm ♿

Seryna (9, C4)   ¥¥¥¥
Japanese
No less than three restaurants under one roof: the **Seryna Honten** (main store) serving shabu-shabu and sukiyaki; **Mon Cher Ton Ton** specialises in Kōbe beef and **Kani Seryna** does crab. Some of the best luxury food Japan has to offer in elegant, if musty, foreigner-friendly surroundings. A longtime favourite of Tokyo expats and the odd stray gangster.
✉ Minato-ku, Roppongi 3-12-2
☎ 3402 1051
🚇 Hibiya line to Roppongi, exit 3
🕐 noon-11pm

Spago (9, C4)   ¥¥¥
American
Wolfgang Puck's paean to Californian cuisine. Yet even this bastion of Beverley Hills excess has had to come to terms with economic realities and cut prices. Nice sunny lunch area.
✉ Minato-ku, Roppongi 5-7-8
☎ 3423 4025
🚇 Hibiya line to Roppongi, exit 3
🕐 11.30am-2pm, 6-10pm

Okonomiyaki – *a favourite fast food at street festivals. In restaurants, it's strictly do-it-yourself.*

SHIBUYA

Fungo (5, C2) ¥
Cafe
Pleasant, handily located sandwich shop and cafe where the sandwiches are excellent. You wont find any odd sweet fillings here (such as strawberries) as is sometimes the case with Tokyo bakeries. Fresh burgers, espresso coffee and American micro-brewed beers are also served here.

✉ Shibuya-ku, Udagawachō 15-1, Parco 3, 3F
☎ 3477 8795
🚇 Hanzōmon & Ginza lines to Shibuya, exits 3 & 6
🕐 10am-9pm ♿ V

Kantipur (5, E3) ¥¥
Nepali
This Nepali restaurant seems to borrow a lot from India, but the food's good and the welcome friendly. Try their cashew and raisin naan bread. It's just south of the Kirin City beer hall, set back from the street.

✉ Shibuya-ku, Sakuragaoka 16-6, Sunrise Sakuragaoka Bldg, B1F
☎ 3770 5358
🚇 Yamanote line to Shibuya, south exit

🕐 11.30am-3pm, 5-11pm V

New York Kitchen (5, B3) ¥
Cafe
Not exactly 'New York', as you don't get harangued by the staff for taking too long to choose, but a good lunch stop with real bagels, a good choice of salads and excellent espresso coffee. There's a choice of eat in or take out.

✉ Shibuya-ku, Jinnan 1-17-5 ☎ 5457 7755
🚇 Hanzōmon & Ginza lines to Shibuya, exits 6 & 7
🕐 11am-11pm ♿ V

Reikyō (5, D2) ¥¥
Taiwanese
Believe it or not, this place is even smokier and more raucous than Tainan Taami. There's no English signage outside, so look for a triangular red-brick building crammed with partying Tokyoites.

✉ Shibuya-ku, Dōgenzaka 2-23-18
☎ 3461 4220
🚇 Hanzōmon & Ginza lines to Shibuya, exit 1
🕐 Fri-Wed noon-2pm, 5pm-1am

Sakana-tei (5, D1) ¥¥
Izakaya
Looks more like a concrete bomb shelter than an izakaya, but the excellent food and drink more than make up for the architectural aberration. The emphasis here is on good-quality sake and simple but tasty cuisine.

✉ Shibuya-ku, Dogenzaka 2-23-15 Koike Bldg, 4F
☎ 3780 1313
🚇 Hanzōmon & Ginza lines to Shibuya, exit 1
🕐 Mon-Sat 5.30pm-1.30am

Tainan Taami (5, E2) ¥¥
Taiwanese
Smoky and raucous – and that's just the staff. Good Taiwanese fare to be found here, right in the heart of Shibuya. You'll need to order several dishes to fill up at any of their branches across the city.

✉ Shibuya-ku, Dōgenzaka 1-17-6
☎ 3464 7544
🚇 Yamanote line to Shibuya, south exit
🕐 Mon-Sat 11am-2pm, 5pm-2am

Late-Night Eats
Feeling peckish in the early hours? Seek out a *yatai*, one of the portable street stalls that set up around the major stations after dusk, and stay open until the early hours. Rāmen noodles are a popular choice.

Oliver Strewe

SHINJUKU

Court Lodge
(4, D3)   ¥¥
Sri Lankan
Good value and authentic Sri Lankan fare can be found in what looks like a coffee shop from outside. The lentil curry and *dotamba* (pancake-like bread) are especially good. There are branches in Meguro and Nakano.
✉ Shinjuku-ku, Shinjuku 3-8-2, Cross Bldg, B1F
☎ 3376 7733
🚇 Marunouchi & Toei Shinjuku lines to Shinjuku-sanchōme, exit C5 🕐 Mon-Sat 11am-midnight, Sun 5-11pm ♿ V

Daikokuya (4, C5)   ¥
Shabu-shabu & Sukiyaki
All-you-can-eat *yakiniku* (Korean barbecue), shabu-shabu and sukiyaki courses bring in the students, making this a good place to get wrecked with the younger locals.
✉ Shinjuku-ku, Kabukichō 1-27-5, Nakadai Bldg, 4F
☎ 3202 7272
🚉 Yamanote line to Shinjuku, Kabukichō exit 🕐 Mon-Fri 5-11.30pm, Sat-Sun 3pm-midnight

Keika Kumamoto Rāmen (4, C5)   ¥¥
Rāmen
This nationally famous rāmen shop, specialising in Kyūshū-style pork broth-based noodles, is currently taking Tokyo by storm. Try the *chāshū-men* noodles with sliced pork. Expect to queue during peak hours. There's no English sign outside,

but it's the only rāmen restaurant located in the area.
✉ Shinjuku-ku, Shinjuku 3-7-2
☎ 3354 4591
🚇 Marunouchi & Toei Shinjuku lines to Shinjuku-sanchōme, exit C4
🚉 Yamanote line to Shinjuku, east exit
🕐 11am-10.45pm ♿

Kurumaya (4, B4) ¥¥¥
Teppanyaki
An elegant spot (at least for east Shinjuku) where the seafood and steak sets are excellent value. Highly recommended is the *ise ebi* (Japanese lobster). There's no English signage outside, but it's directly across from Kirin City beer hall.
✉ Shinjuku-ku, Kabukichō 2-37-1
☎ 3232 0301
🚉 Yamanote line to Shinjuku, Kabukichō exit 🕐 11.30am-2.30pm, 5-10.30pm

New York Grill
(4, D1)   ¥¥¥
International
Fancy some power dining in the sky? This place on the 52nd floor of the Park Hyatt Tower stands out from the crowd with its hearty portions of steak and seafood, not to mention the drop-dead view. Warm up with a few cocktails at the adjoining New York Bar. It's also well worth getting up in time for the Sunday brunch.
✉ Shinjuku-ku, Nishi-Shinjuku 3-7-1-2, Park Hyatt Tokyo, 52F
☎ 5323 3458

🚇 Toei Shinjuku line to Shinjuku, exit 7
🕐 11.30am-midnight

Shinjuku Negishi
(4, A4)   ¥
Japanese, Country Cooking
A very rustic hang-out for carnivores only. The beef tongue and beef stew sets are tasty stuff at this cosy Japanese country-fare specialist in the heart of modern Tokyo. Not too far from the Shinjuku Prince Hotel.
✉ Shinjuku-ku, Kabukichō 2-45-2
☎ 3232 8020
🚉 Yamanote line to Shinjuku, east exit
🕐 11am-3pm, 5-10.30pm

Tenkaippin
(4, A4)   ¥
Rāmen
Specify *'kotteri'* for thick soup or *'asari'* for thin, at this popular noodle joint that originally hails from Kyoto. Weight-watchers and health fiends should not cross the threshold. Even the 'light' soup is sorely calorie-laden. You'll need to look for the red lanterns and red-and-white decor.
✉ Shinjuku-ku, Kabukichō 1-14-3, 103 Tokyo Bldg, 1F & 2F
☎ 3232 7454
🚇 Marunouchi & Toei Shinjuku lines to Shinjuku-sanchōme, exits B11, B12 & B13
🚉 Yamanote line to Shinjuku, Kabukichō exit 🕐 Mon-Thurs 11am-4am, Fri-Sat 10am-7am, Sun 10am-1am ♿

UENO

Echikatsu
(10, E1) ¥¥¥
Sukiyaki
Sukiyaki and shabu-shabu in the exquisite surroundings of a grand old Japanese house. Many rooms overlook small gardens. The staff don't speak English, but will make an genuine effort to communicate. Reservations are, however, necessary.
✉ **Bunkyō-ku, Yushima 2-31-23** ☎ **3811 5293**
🚇 **Chiyoda line to Yushima, exit 5**
🕐 **Mon-Sat 5-9.30pm**

Ganko-zushi Ueno Honten (10, D3) ¥¥
Sushi
Relaxed sushi restaurant that spawned a successful nationwide chain. They're used to foreigners asking 'Am I supposed to eat this part?' Good value.
✉ **Taitō-ku, Ueno 4-9-6, Nagafuji Bldg, 6F** ☎ **5688 8845**
🚇 **Ginza & Hibiya lines to Ueno, exits 4, 5a & 5b**
🚉 **Yamanote line to Ueno, Shinobazu exit**
🕐 **11.30am-3pm, 4.30-11pm** ♿

Izu-ei Honten
(10, E3) ¥¥
Unagi
Beautifully presented, authentic Japanese eel cuisine. An excellent spot to take Japanese friends or colleagues to dinner. There is a limited picture menu. Look for the black building with a small pine tree and waterfall out the front.
✉ **Taitō-ku, Ueno 2-12-22** ☎ **3831 0954**
🚇 **Chiyoda line to Yushima, exit 2**
🚉 **Keisei train line to Keisei-Ueno, main exit**
🕐 **11am-10pm**

Kameya Issui-tei
(10, D3) ¥¥¥
Kaiseki
Elegant Kameya serves high-class food in very pleasant surroundings. There's no English spoken, but the daily lunch set is displayed outside. In the evening, you'll need a phrasebook, or just take the plunge.
✉ **Taitō-ku, Ueno 2-13-2** ☎ **3831 0912**
🚇 **Ginza & Hibiya lines to Ueno, exit 5b**
🚉 **Keisei line to Keisei-Ueno, main exit; Yamanote line to Ueno, Shinobazu exit**
🕐 **11.30am-9.20pm**

Maguroyā-san
(10, C5) ¥¥
Tuna
Or 2001 things to do with a dead tuna. *Maguro* means tuna, and if it can be made from that creature, it's probably on the menu, including exotic and tasty *maguro gyōza* (tuna-filled dumplings). A true rarity in that it is non-smoking during lunch hours.
✉ **Taitō-ku, Higashi-Ueno 4-8-3**
☎ **3844 2732**
🚇 **Ginza & Hibiya lines to Ueno, exit 1**

🚉 **Yamanote line to Ueno, Asakusa exit**
🕐 **Mon-Sat 11am-3pm, 5pm-11pm** ♿

Samrat (10, D3) ¥
Indian
Samrat serves the usual Indian curries and curry sets. Closer to the station, it's just around the corner from the popular foreigner's bar Hub. There's usually a tout outside beckoning people in.
✉ **Taitō-ku, Ueno 4-8-9, Oak Bldg, 2F** ☎ **3770 7275**
🚇 **Ginza & Hibiya lines to Ueno, exits 5a & 5b**
🚉 **Yamanote line to Ueno, Shinobazu exit**
🕐 **11am-10pm** ♿ **V**

Ueno Yabu Soba
(10, D4) ¥
Soba
Top-class soba noodles mean you can put up with the chain-restaurant decor and the seen-it-all couldn't-care-less staff. The most substantial dish is the *tenseiro* set, which includes tempura.
✉ **Taitō-ku, Ueno 6-9-16** ☎ **3831 4728**
🚇 **Ginza & Hibiya lines to Ueno, exits 4, 5a & 5b** 🚉 **Yamanote line to Ueno, Hirokōji exit**
🕐 **Thurs-Tues 11.30am-8pm** ♿ **V**

Worth a Trip
It's a bit of a hike to **Sasagin** (Shibuya-ku, Uehara 1-32-15 ☎ 5454 3715;.Chiyoda line to Yoyogi-kōen, exit 1; Odakyū line to Yoyogi-Uehara, south exit; Mon-Sat 5-11.30pm), possibly Tokyo's best value mid-range restaurant. It's classy but relaxed ambience, excellent food and top-notch sake make the trek out to the semi-wilds of Yoyogi-Uehara well worthwhile. Turn right at the station exit, and it's several minutes' walk on your left.

entertainment

It isn't hard to find something to keep you out of trouble in Tokyo. Or get you into it. Whether its kabuki or karaoke, hot-spring hopping or pub-crawling, the Big Umeboshi – the Giant Sour Plum – has it all. There's no season – it's full-on big-city hyperactivity all year round. And of course that means eating and drinking.

Above all drinking. Tokyo loves to party. The centre of the maelstrom is Roppongi, with its gaijin-filled bars and clubs. Ginza and Akasaka are more exclusive, but throw up some interesting options. Shibuya hops 24 hours and east Shinjuku has a bar or club to cater to every taste, no matter how bizarre.

Last Drinks

It's overdue. Every Tokyo resident's worst fear is *daishinsai*, the gigantic earthquake that soothsayers and seismologists alike agree will level the city. It could happen at any moment. Perhaps this accounts for the colossal amount of drinking that goes on? That's Yin and Yang. No earthquakes, no hot-springs.

What's On

The local English-language papers are the best source for the latest music and theatre performances around Tokyo. *Metropolis* (weekly) and *Tokyo Journal* (monthly) can be found in book stores (p. 66). Tokyo's contemporary theatre scene is effectively off-limits to non-Japanese speakers. Live contemporary music venues are called 'live house' in Tokyo, whether it's a grungy basement hole or a top-floor lounge.

John McInnes

The spectacle of traditional archery, twice a year at Meiji-jingū shrine, Harajuku

SPECIAL EVENTS

January

New Year's Day – the first shrine visit of the year; eating of buckwheat noodles

Dezome-shiki – 6 January; excellent photo opportunities at this firefighter's festival in front of Tokyo Big Sight, Ōdaiba

Hatsu-basho – sumō tournament at Kokugikan

Seijin-no-hi – 15 January; traditional display of archery at Meiji-jingū

February

Setsubun – 13 February; demon-expelling, bean-throwing ceremonies, best experienced at Sensō-ji, Asakusa

March

Girls' day festival – 3 March; a doll fair is held in Asakusabashi

March/April

Hanami – cherry-blossom viewing across the city during outdoor picnics and parties

April

Jibeta Matsuri – 15 April; Kawasaki festival that celebrates the vanquishing of a sharp-toothed demon residing in a young maiden, by means of an iron phallus

Kamakura Matsuri – 2nd Sunday; week of festival celebrations centred around Tsurugaoka Hachiman-gū in Kamakura

May

Natsu-basho Sumo Tournament – wrestlers settle grudges smouldering since January at Kokugikan

Asakusa Sanja Matsuri – raucous festival in and around Asakusa-jinja shrine

June

Japan Derby – Tokyo Racecourse – tens of thousands flock to the races

Iris viewing – across the city, especially at Meiji-jingū

July

Sumida-gawa fireworks display – last weekend in July; the most popular *hanabi* of the year

August

Fuji Rock Festival – 3-day event that draws top international and local acts

O-bon – 13-15 August; Buddhist Feast of the Dead when Tokyoites return to their parents' home to welcome the visiting spirits of their ancestors

Asakusa Samba Festival – the Brazilian community dances in the street

September

Sumo Tournament Aki-basho – the last battle of the year at Kokugikan

October/November

Meiji Reidaisai – 30 October-3 November; displays of traditional horseback archery by riders at Meiji-jingū shrine

Tokyo International Film Festival

November

Shichi-go-san festival – 15 November; for children aged 3, 5 and 7

December

All-Japan Kendo Championships

Emperor's Birthday – 23 December; the Imperial Palace grounds are opened to the public

New Year's Eve – 31 December; at midnight the freezing populace flock to Shinto shrines to toll the bell 108 times to atone for their past year's sins; Meiji-jingū shrine is especially festive

BARS & PUBS

Drinking is the Japanese national pastime, and Tokyo offers infinite possibilities whether you're up for the occasional G&T, or a certifiable alcoholic. *Izakaya,* which crop up often in the Places to Eat section, are half-restaurant, half-pub and an unmissable Tokyo experience. Try at least one.

Abbey Road (9, B3)
If you've never seen a Japanese Beatles-cover band, you should. With such favourites as 'Gotta Get You Into My Raifu', and 'Rub Me Do', it's guaranteed to be fun.
✉ Minato-ku, Roppongi 4-11-5, Roppongi Annex Bldg, B1F
☎ 3402 0017
Ⓜ Toei Ōedo & Hibiya lines to Roppongi, exit 4
🕐 Mon-Sat 6pm-1am

Agave (9, C3)
Far more varieties of tequila and mezcales than are good for the body and soul at this pleasant, oft-crowded subterranean slice of Mexico. Beware of the lethal cocktails.
✉ Minato-ku, Roppongi 7-15-10, Clover Bldg, B1F
☎ 3497 0229
Ⓜ Hibiya & Toei Ōedo lines to Roppongi, exit 2
🕐 Mon-Fri 6.30pm-2am, Sat-Sun 6.30pm-4am

Bodeguita (9, C4)
A centre of Tokyo's booming Latin craze. As soon as everyone's finished eating (there's a good selection of none-too-expensive Latin dishes) they clear away the tables and it's salsa time – either join in or be crushed.
✉ Minato-ku, Roppongi 3-14-7
☎ 3796 0232
ⓔ www.bodeguita.com
Ⓜ Toei Ōedo & Hibiya lines to Roppongi, exit 3

🕐 Sun-Wed 6pm-1am, Thurs-Sat 6pm-late

Club 328 (9, D1)
Also known as San-ni-ppa, this is an R&B refuge from Roppongi madness – just up the road in Nishi-Azabu. The young but laid-back patrons start to groove around midnight.
✉ Minato-ku, Nishi-Azabu 3-24-20
☎ 3401 4968
ⓔ www.02.246.ne.jp/~azabu328
Ⓜ Toei Ōedo & Hibiya lines to Roppongi, exit 1
🕐 8pm-5am

Dusk Till Dawn (9, C4)
The name says it all really. It's a popular hang-out that usually fills up during the happy hour, then keeps filling up throughout the night. Presumably not everyone's there for the

Cajun fish 'n' chips.
✉ Minato-ku, Roppongi 3-13-8, Zonan Bldg, 2F
☎ 5771 2258
Ⓜ Toei Ōedo & Hibiya lines to Roppongi, exit 3
🕐 Mon-Sat 5pm-5am; happy hour 6-9pm

Fujiya Honten (5, E3)
Legendary old *tachi-nomi* (stand-up-and-drink place) on the south-west side of Shibuya station. This is fascinating, not-a-little-rough bare-light-bulb territory. Wash down the nibbles with beer and sake at rock bottom prices, and prepare to be engaged in oft-friendly, oft-slurred conversation. Ladies should probably ponder whether they really want to drop in.
✉ Shibuya-ku, Sakuragaokachō 1-2-3, B1F ☎ 3461 2128

Michael Taylor

Well-stocked bars are all the rage in Roppongi.

🚋 **Yamanote line to Shibuya**, south exit
🕐 5-9.30pm

Gas Panic Club (9, C4)
A slightly, very slightly, upmarket version of its rowdy progenitor, Gas Panic bar. You're marginally less likely to get decked by testosterone-crazed military personnel here. The GP lowest common denominator, cheap-booze craziness can be fun if you're in the mood. Just don't look the person next to you in the eye at the bar. And that's the girl.
✉ **Minato-ku, Roppongi 3-15-24**
☎ 3402 7054
🚇 **Toei Ōedo & Hibiya lines to Roppongi**, exit 3
🕐 8pm-6am

Drinking Etiquette

If you're out for a few drinks, remember that you're expected to keep the drinks of your companions topped up. Don't fill your own glass: wait for someone to do this for you. It's polite to hold the glass with both hands while it is being filled. The Japanese equivalent of cheers is 'Kampai!'

Geronimo (9, C3)
An unpretentious, popular shot bar that gets packed out with all sorts of off-work Tokyo expats and a few of their Japanese associates. At happy hour (6-8pm) all drinks are half price.
✉ **Minato-ku, Roppongi 7-14-10, 2F**
☎ 3478 7449

🚇 **Toei Ōedo & Hibiya lines to Roppongi**, exit 4a
🕐 7pm-5am

G-Martini's (9, C5)
Complete with lava lamps, Austin Powers decor and a menu of more than 30 generously-proportioned martinis. The only thing to remind you that you're in Roppongi not Cannes circa 1966 is, naturally, the Shag Room. It's across from the Axis building.
✉ **Minato-ku, Roppongi 5-18-21, Five Plaza Bldg, 4F**
☎ 3588 6147
📧 **www.gmartinis.com**
🚇 **Toei Ōedo & Hibiya lines to Roppongi**, exit 3
🕐 7pm-6am

Highlander (8, E5)
Low on glitz, high on quality, the Hotel Ōkura's bar is the perfect place to wind down after a strenuous business day, or wind up for an evening out in the bars and restaurants of upmarket Akasaka.
✉ **Minato-ku, Toranomon 2-10-4, Hotel Ōkura**
☎ 3505 6077
🚇 **Hibiya line to Kamiyachō**, exit 2
🕐 Mon-Sat 11.30am-1am, Sun 11.30am-midnight

Hobgoblin Tokyo (8, C3)
Far better than your average Tokyo Brit-pub replica. Run by an Oxfordshire brewery, it has good pub fare and excellent imported microbrews so try the Black Wych stout. It stays open until the early hours, unlike many places this end of town.
✉ **Minato-ku, Akasaka 2-3-19, Tamondo Bldg, B1F**

☎ 3585 3681
📧 **www.hobgoblin-tokyo.com** 🚇 **Chiyoda line to Akasaka**, exit 2; **Ginza & Namboku lines to Tameike-sannō**, exit 9 🕐 11.30am-late

Kamiya (11, D4)
Splendid old place, once popular with the Tokyo literati, that hasn't changed much since it was founded in 1880. The 1st floor is a beer hall where you pay for drinks as you enter. Its best-known offering is the brandy-based cocktail *denki-bran*. There are restaurants on the 2nd and 3rd floors.
✉ **Taito-ku, Asakusa 1-1-1** ☎ 3841 5400
🚇 **Ginza line to Asakusa**, exit 3
🕐 Wed-Mon 11.30am-10pm

Las Chicas (6, E4)
Internet terminals and terminal trendiness mix at the Harajuku bar-restaurant that is rapidly becoming a Tokyo institution. Be careful not to drip your walnut gnocchi on your designer trousers.
✉ **Shibuya-ku, Jingūmae 5-47-6**
☎ 3407 6865
🚇 **Chiyoda, Ginza & Hanzōmon lines to Omote-sandō**, exit B2
🕐 11am-11pm

Mix (6, D5)
Small, smoky, pokey hole-in-the-wall, as friendly as it is crowded. Reggae and hip-hop predominate, and even if the rest of Roppongi is dead, Mix won't be.
✉ **Minato-ku, Kita-Aoyama 3-6-19, B1**
☎ 3797 1313
📧 **www.at-mix.com**

🚇 Chiyoda, Ginza & Hanzōmon lines to Omote-sandō, exit B4
🕐 6-11pm

Motown House 1 & 2
(9, C4) The impolite call it 'ho town', but on the pick-up front it's no worse (or better?) than its neighbours. And since it expanded from 1 to 1 & 2, it can actually be quite relaxed.
✉ **Minato-ku, Roppongi 3-11-5**
☎ 5474 4605
🚇 Toei Ōedo & Hibiya lines to Roppongi, exit 3
🕐 7pm-late

New York Bar (4, D1)
Splendid, civilised cocktail bar up in the higher stratosphere, both literally and socially, of the Park Hyatt in west Shinjuku. Great date-spot, great drinks. Equally magnificent views, as long as you go easy on the Long Island Iced Teas.
✉ **Shinjuku-ku, Nishi-Shinjuku 3-7-1-2**
☎ 5323 3458
🖥 www.parkhyatt tokyo.com
🚇 Marunouchi & Toei Shinjuku lines to Shinjuku, exit 7
🚃 Yamanote line to Shinjuku, west exit
🕐 Sun-Wed 5pm-midnight, Thurs-Sat 5pm-1am

Old Imperial Bar
(12, G3) An impossibly dignified hotel bar over in Hibiya. It's the sort of place where you'd drink your last cognac before jumping off Tokyo Tower, having squandered the family millions on the horses at Ōi race-course.
✉ **Chiyoda-ku, Uchisaiwaichō 1-1-1,**

Chris Mellor

Soak up the bright lights of Shinjuku.

Imperial Hotel
☎ 3504 1111
🚇 Hibiya, Marunouchi & Chiyoda lines to Hibiya, exit A13
🕐 11.30am-midnight

Pink Cow (6, C1)
Favourite bar-cum-hideaway of local and gaijin subversive types who come here to plot artistic revolution. The Friday night barbecue is excellent and the walls, bedecked with customers' work, are never dull. Arty, but far from farty.
✉ **Shibuya-ku, Jingūmae 1-10-1**
☎ 5411 6777
🚇 Chiyoda line to Meiji-jingūmae, exit 3
🚃 Yamanote line to

Harajuku, Omote-sandō exit 🕐 Tue-Sun 5pm-late

Salsa Sudada (9, B3)
Salsa is big in Tokyo and this is the place to strut your funky salsa stuff, make no mistake. This long-time favourite of Tokyo's salsa lovers has been revamped and goes from strength to strength. Unless you're prepared to take to the floor, you might as well stay at home.
✉ **Minato-ku, Roppongi 7-13-8, La Palette Bldg, 3F**
☎ 5474 8806
🚇 Toei Ōedo & Hibiya lines to Roppongi, exit 4a
🕐 6pm-6am

More than just sake.

John Ashburne

Scruffy Murphy's
(6, D3) Dust off your *bodhran*, and head over to Omote-sandō for an evening of impromptu Gaelic music and good Irish beer. Murphy's has excellent live bands almost every night of the week.
📮 Shibuya-ku, Jingūmae 6-5-6, Sampou Sogo Bldg, 2F
☎ 3499 3145
🄴 www.geocities.com/scruffymurphystokyo
🄼 Chiyoda line to Meiji-jingūmae, exit 4 🚇 Yamanote line to Harajuku, Omote-sandō exit
🕐 11.30am-late

Smash Hits (3, L4)
Watch your friends wince as you labour through 'I Left my Heart in San Fransisco', or deafen them with the Sid Vicious version of 'My Way'. Excruciating fun of the highest order at this karaoke place with 12,000 English-language choices. The Vapours' hit, 'Turning

Japanese', is a must.
📮 Shibuya-ku, Hiro-o 5-2-26, M2 Hiro-o Bldg, B2F
☎ 3444 0432
🄼 Hibiya line to Hiro-o, exit 1
🕐 7pm-3am

Trading Places (9, C5)
What was that about separating business and pleasure? The Bloomberg news chatters away full-time here, as expat traders come to sink pints and discuss imminent mergers. Not always of the financial variety. Laid-back for this part of town, with de rigeur DJ and big screen showing movies.
📮 Minato-ku, Roppongi 5-16-52, Imperial Roppongi Bldg, B1F
☎ 3589 2442
🄼 Hibiya & Toei Ōedo lines to Roppongi, exit 3
🕐 Mon-Sat 6pm-3am

What the Dickens
(7, B3) This is one of Tokyo's better English-style pubs. It has a pleasant,

spacious feel, and there's usually a band in the corner playing good mellow music. What the Dickens serves filling, hearty pub food and Guinness on tap. What more could you want?
📮 Shibuya-ku, Ebisu-Nishi 1-13-3, Roob 6 Bldg, 4F
☎ 3780 2099
🄼 Hibiya line to Ebisu, exit 2
🚇 Yamanote line to Ebisu, west exit
🕐 Tues-Sat 5pm-2am, Sun 3pm-midnight

Zona Rosa (7, B4)
If Bodeguita hasn't quenched your thirst for all things Latin, go to Zona Rosa for authentic margaritas, Mexican beers and a wholesome variety of Latin (mostly Mexican) food.
📮 Shibuya-ku, Ebisu 1-12-5
☎ 3440 3878
🚇 Yamanote line to Ebisu, east exit
🕐 11.30am-6am

Beer Gardens with Altitude
When temperatures soar, the best way to beat the heat is to head for a rooftop beer garden, usually atop a department store. Up above the crowds and the traffic, it's easy to forget you're in such a hectic city. Many offer all-you-can-eat-and/or-drink specials for around ¥3000 over a set time limit. Of course, rooftop beer gardens are only open in the summer months and closed during rain periods. Try one of the following: **Ikebukuro Parco Tai Tai** (2, B3; ☎ 3987 0552; Parco department store; Ikebukuro station, east exit, 5-10pm), **My City Beer Garden** (4, B3; ☎ 5360 7144; My City, Shinjuku station, My City exit, Sun 4-10pm) or **Shibuya Tōkyū Honten** (5, D3; ☎ 3477 3478; Tōkyū Shibuya department store, Shibuya station, Tōkyū exit; 5-9.30pm).

DANCE CLUBS

Tokyo's club scene is thriving at all hours every day, though places do come and go. It's good to call ahead to check a place still exists. Usually the entrance fee includes one or two 'free' drink tokens.

Blue (3, K4)
Hard to find seriously hip club, with cool interior design and cave-like atmosphere. Mod Tokyo student types come here to flip their collective wigs to acid jazz and house beats. It's quite a walk from central Aoyama, past the Blue Note. Look for a portable sign at street level. It's in the basement.
✉ **Minato-ku, Minami-Aoyama 6-2-9, NYK Bldg, B1F & B2F**
☎ **3797 1591**
Ⓜ **Hibiya line to Hiro-o, exit 3** ⏱ **9pm-5am**
⑤ **¥1500**

Lexington Queen
(9, C4) The place where you are most likely to rub shoulders with Naomi, Claudia and Elton, but this Tokyo institution is well past its prime, despite local celebrity Bill Hersey's ability to pull in the stars
✉ **Minato-ku, Roppongi 3-13-14, Third Goto Bldg, B1F**
☎ **3401 1661**
ⓔ **www.lexington-queen.com**
Ⓜ **Toei Ōedo & Hibiya lines to Roppongi, exit 3**
⏱ **8pm-5am**
⑤ **men ¥4000/3000**

Luners (9, E5)
Palatial new club with lasers and the works that hosts a variety of events, including regular gay and lesbian nights
✉ **Minato-ku, Azabu-jūban 1-4-5, Fukao Bldg, 1F & B1F**
☎ **3586 6383**
ⓔ **www.luners.co.jp**
Ⓜ **Toei Ōedo line to Azabu-jūban, exit 7**
⏱ **Thurs-Sat 8pm-late**
⑤ **¥3500**

Maniac Love (6, E5)
Techno mecca that really comes into its own around 5am Sunday morning, when the after-hours crowd come to strut their weird and funky stuff. In best Aoyama tradition, it's a pig to find, behind an unmarked steel door in the basement of the Tera A Omote-sandō building.
✉ **Minato-ku, Minami-Aoyama 5-10-6, B1F**
☎ **3406 1166**
ⓔ **www.maniaclove.com**
Ⓜ **Chiyoda, Ginza, & Hanzōmon lines to Omote-sandō, exit B1**
⏱ **Thurs-Fri 10pm-5am, Sat 10pm-10am**
⑤ **¥2000-2500**

Velfarre (9, B3)
Mainstream disco the size of a small European nation. Over-the-top decor compensates for the ordinary vibe. Its private after-hours parties though are a different story. Discount cover charge for women some nights.
✉ **Minato-ku, Roppongi 7-14-22**
☎ **3402 8000**
Ⓜ **Toei Ōedo & Hibiya lines to Roppongi, exit 4a**
⏱ **Thurs-Sun 6pm-midnight**
⑤ **¥2000-3500**

Yellow (9, D1)
Located by the Nishi-Azabu crossing, this is one of the most progressive and hippest places in town. Everything from house to acid jazz, Brazil jazz to techno and foreign DJ nights are featured at Yellow.
✉ **Minato-ku, Nishi-Azabu 1-10-11, Cesaurus Bldg, B1F & B2F**
☎ **3479 0690**
ⓔ **www.space-lab-yellow.com** Ⓜ **Toei Ōedo & Hibiya lines to Roppongi, exit 2**
⏱ **8.30pm-late**
⑤ **¥2500-3500**

Closing Chaos
By the late 1990s, Tokyo had developed a vibrant and diverse club scene. In 1999, a series of club closures by police left punters stunned on pavements outside. Rumours were rife. Was it the newly appointed Azabu police chief? Commercial redevelopment planned in the area?

Clubs such as **Yellow**, **Luners** (p. 93) and **Club 328** (p. 89) re-opened shortly after a spell of uncertainty. Was it merely a policy of containment (as all are located outside the unofficial 'entertainment' district along Gaien-Higashi-dōri)?

LIVE MUSIC VENUES

Blue Note (3, K3)

Serious cognoscenti roll up at Tokyo's prime jazz spot, in Aoyama, prepared to shell out much moolah on the likes of Maceo Parker, Sergio Mendes and Chick Corea.
✉ **Minato-ku, Minami-Aoyama 6-3-16**
☎ **5485 0088**
🚇 **Chiyoda, Ginza, & Hanzōmon lines to Omote-sandō, exit B1**
🕐 **stage 1 at 7pm, stage 2 at 9.30pm**
💲 **from ¥6000**

Club Quattro (5, C2)

Another showcase venue for local and international artists. Although it's located in the heart of Shibuya, it's actually in a department store building (and there's a lift) which makes for a slightly bizarre entry.
✉ **Shibuya-ku, Hachiko**
☎ **3477 8750**
🚉 **Yamanote line to Shibuya, Hachiko exit**
🕐 **7pm-late**
💲 **varies**

Keeping a different beat in Harajuku.

Martin Moos

Liquid Room (4, A4)

Some of the world's greatest performers have graced the stage of the Liquid Room, from The Flaming Lips to Linton Kwesi Johnson. It's a long way to the top (there's no lift), but once up there, the venue is comfortable and well-designed. Also renowned for international and local club nights.
✉ **Shinjuku-ku, Kabukichō 1-20-1, Humax Pavilion 7F**
☎ **3200 6831**
🇪 **www.liquidroom .net** 🚇 **Marunouchi line to Shinjuku, exit B13** 🚉 **Yamanote line to Shinjuku, Kabukichō exit** 🕐 **7pm-late**
💲 **varies**

Milk (7, B3)

One of Tokyo's best small live clubs, featuring international punk, rock and alternative, along with some of Tokyo's better underground acts. This is a cool space, with three underground levels and a crowd of weirdly wonderful local characters. In the basement below What the Dickens pub.
✉ **Shibuya-ku, Ebisu-Nishi 1-13-3, Roob 6 Bldg, B1F** ☎ **5458 2826** 🇪 **www.milk-tokyo.com** 🚇 **Hibiya line to Ebisu, exit 2**
🕐 **8pm-4am** 💲 **around ¥1000**

Shinjuku Pit Inn (9, C5)

Doesn't pull the really big names but still plenty of good jazz acts here.
✉ **Shinjuku-ku, Shinjuku 2-12-4**
☎ **3354 2024**
🚇 **Toei Shinjuku line to Shinjuku-sanchōme, exits C5 & C8**
🕐 **2.30-10.30pm**
💲 **¥3000-10,000**

What's in a Name?

Tokyo is home to some of the most original pop, rock or punk band names. Currently playing on the music scene are Doing Life, No Faction Japs, The Spy 'C' Dildog, Lump of Mind, Tangy Burp (with Donut Man), Illmatic Head Lock, Asian Kung Fu Generation, and, this observer's favourite, Ex-Asshole.

John Ashburne

THEATRE, DANCE & TRADITIONAL ARTS

Bunraku is a puppet performance unique to Japan. Each puppet is half to two-thirds life-size and is operated by three hooded, visible puppeteers. A single narrator, standing on a dias to one side, intones the story using a different voice for each of the characters.

Nō began over 600 years ago as an art performance for court and relies on understatement through stark sets and subtle masks to focus attention on the performers. Only two performers – *waki* or 'one who watches' and *shite* or 'one who acts' – are essential in nō. The waki unmasks the shite, who is never what he or she seems to be. Often the shite is a ghost whose spirit remains after a past tragedy. Once unmasked, the shite dances in the second act to reveal his or her true identity.

Ginza Nō-gakudō

(12, G4) This theatre is only five minutes on foot from Ginza subway station. Turn right onto Sotobori-dōri in the direction of Shimbashi at the Sukiyabashi crossing; look for the theatre on the left.

✉ Chūō-ku, Ginza 6-5-15 ☎ 3571 0197
🚇 Ginza, Marunouchi, Toei Asakusa, & Hibiya lines to Ginza, exit B7
⑤ around ¥5000
🕐 vary

Kanze Nō-gakudō

(5, C1) This theatre is attached to one of the traditional schools of nō. By far the most exciting are the occasional outdoor night performances of Takigi Nō, where the masked actors are illuminated by huge burning torches. Very atmospheric.

✉ Shibuya-ku, Shoto 1-16-4
☎ 3469 6241
🚉 Yamanote line to Shibuya, Hachikō exit
🕐 vary ⑤ from ¥3000

Kokuritsu Geikijō Theatre

(8, A5) Astonishingly life-like puppetry. Performances take place in Tokyo in February, May, September and December.

✉ Chiyoda-ku, Hayabusa-chō 4-1
☎ 3265 7411

🚇 Hanzōmon line to Hanzōmon, exit 1
🕐 tickets 10am-6pm, performances 11.30am & 5pm ⑤ ¥5800

Kokuritsu Nō-gakudō

(3, H3) Also known as the National Nō Theatre, this performance venue is in Sendagaya on the Chūō line. There are performances here on weekends only.

✉ Shibuya-ku, Sendagaya 4-18-1
☎ 3423 1331
🚉 Chūō line to Sendagaya, west exit
🕐 vary
⑤ ¥2800-5600

Oh Nō!

This is the polite way to refer to Japan's ancient theatrical art, nō, pictured left. Alas, that's often the reaction of both Japanese and foreigners, who find it repetitive and impenetrable. In spite of this, nō continues to attract large audiences. Be warned.

JNTO

GAY & LESBIAN TOKYO

Shinjuku, in particular, is the main area for gay and lesbian bars and clubs. Many clubs now have mixed nights so for latest events check out the street press. The Annual (usually in May) Tokyo International Lesbian and Gay Film and Video Festival takes to screens across the city and is definitely worth a look. Contact festival organisers (☎ 5380 5767 e lgff@tokyo.office.ne.jp; l-gff.gender.ne.jp/2001/e/index.html) for full program dates and details. *Tokyo Journal's* Cityscope section sometimes has a special insert called 'Tokyo Out'. Also read Gay & Lesbian Travellers (p. 117) for further information.

Arty Farty (4, C5)
In spite of the name, this is one place where anyone can comfortably walk in and have a good time. Meeting people here is easy and it's a good place to learn about the area's other possibilities.
✉ **Shinjuku-ku, Shinjuku 2-4-17**
☎ **3356 5388**
e **www.arty-farty.net**
🚇 **Toei Shinjuku & Marunouchi lines to Shinjuku-sanchōme, exit B2**

⏲ **Mon-Sat 5pm-5am, Sun 4pm-5am**

Club Ace (3, G3)
An easy-going place for both men and women to relax, enjoy some chill-out tracks and lounge on velvet sofas. American-run, this is a good place to meet fellow out-of-towners.
✉**Shinjuku-ku, Shinjuku 2-14-6**
☎ **3352 6297**
🚇 **Toei Shinjuku & Marunouchi lines to Shinjuku-sanchōme,**

exit B2 ⏲Mon-Sun 8pm-4am

Club Dragon (3, G3)
This is the hard-core leather centre of Tokyo. It's for men only with heavy techno, all-male videos and a back room. Wear at least a leather belt and prepare for an adventurous night.
✉ **Shinjuku-ku, Shinjuku 2-14-4 Accord Bldg**
☎ **3341 0606**
🚇 **Toei Shinjuku & Marunouchi lines to Shinjuku-sanchōme, exit C8**
⏲ **Fri-Sat 9pm-5am, Tue-Thurs & Sun 8pm-5am**

Kinswomyn (4, B5)
This is a friendly, popular lesbian bar run by well-known activist Tara, on the 3rd floor of the Dai-ichi Tenka building, off Yasukuni-dōri. Perfect for visitors as English is spoken.
✉ **Shinjuku-ku, Shinjuku 2-15-10**
☎ **3354 8720**
🚇 **Toei Shinjuku & Marunouchi lines to Shinjuku-sanchōme, exit B7** ⏲ **Wed-Mon 8pm-4am**

Luners (9, E5) See Dance Clubs (p. 93)

Cinemas
Tokyo's cinemas are concentrated in Ginza, Shibuya and Shinjuku. Most show Western films with Japanese subtitles, or domestic titles without English. Some smaller cinemas show funky, limited-release and art-house favourites, and classic Japanese movies with English subtitles.

Ticket prices, however, are probably the highest in the world, ranging from ¥1800 to ¥2300. If you plan ahead, tickets can be bought at certain outlets at discounted prices. Typically, a ¥1800 ticket will cost ¥1300 or less this way.

Cine Amuse East/West (5, C2; Shibuya-ku, Dōgenzaka 23; ☎ 3496 2888; Yamanote line to Shibuya, Hachikō exit; 10am-11pm; ¥1800/1000) is Tokyo's most *gaijin*-friendly cinema (equipped with two screens and an excellent sound system) as it has regular screenings of Japanese movies subtitled in English, in the small but comfy space.

PUBLIC BATHS & HOT SPRINGS

Taking a bath may not sound like your idea of an evening's entertainment, but a good *sentō* (public bath) or *onsen* (hot spring) is more than just a place to wash; it's a place to relax, socialise and forget about the world outside.

Sentō is a vanishing institution in Tokyo, and it's worth visiting one while it's still possible. The following are a few of Tokyo's more accessible sentō and onsen.

Azabu-Jūban Onsen
(9, E4) This is an upmarket hot-spring bath popular with visitors to Tokyo. Don't be alarmed – the rust-coloured water is said to have curative powers.
✉ Minato-ku, Azabu-jūban 1-5-22
☎ 3405 4670
🚇 Toei Ōedo line to Azabu-jūban, exit 7
🕐 Wed-Mon 11am-9pm ⑤ ¥1260/630 ♨

Rokuryu (10, B1)
Boil away travel fatigue at this hot-spring bathhouse. The bubbling amber water is good for you. It's near the Suigetsu Hotel.
✉ Taitō-ku, Ikenohata 3-4-20 ☎ 3821 3826
🚇 Yamanote line to Ueno, Ikenohata exit
🕐 Tues-Sun 3.30-11pm ⑤ ¥400/180 ♨

Koshino-yu (9, E4)
Downstairs, in the same building, this simple place is popular with locals and is also one of the few true *onsen* within the Tokyo city limits. It's a good introduction to the pleasures of a hot-spring bath.
✉ Minato-ku, Azabu-jūban 1-5-21
☎ 3401 8324
🚇 Toei Ōedo line to Azabu-jūban, exit 7
🕐 Wed-Mon 3-11pm ⑤ ¥400/180 ♨

Making a Splash in the Sentō
As much for gossip as for hygiene, the sentō is a great place for strengthening social bonds in Tokyo. Divided into men's and women's sections, you head for the appropriate changeroom and pay the fee to an attendant. In the changing room, place your clothes in one of the wicker or plastic baskets and your toiletries in a *senmenki* (common washbowl). With the basket in a locker, you're ready for your bath.

Before you step into the bath, you'll need to wash thoroughly at the banks of low showers and water spigots that line the walls. Grab a low stool and wash away, making sure you remove all soap so as not to cloud the water. Now choose your tub. At good sentō baths you can choose between a hot tub, scalding tub, cold tub, whirlpool bath, sauna and, best of all, electric bath (which is supposed to simulate the sensation experienced when swimming with electric eels). If you soak everything just right, you'll achieve the state of *yud-dako* or 'boiled octopus'.

Craig McLachlan

SPECTATOR SPORTS

Baseball

Japan is baseball crazy and trip to a Japanese ballpark is truly a cultural experience. The home team's fans often turn up in matching *happi* half-length coats and perform intricate cheering rituals in perfect unison led by

Tokyo Dome: worth the trip

special cheerleaders, one for each section, who seem to make a job out of whipping fans into a well-ordered frenzy. **Tokyo Dome** (3, E6; Bunkyō-ku, Kōraku 1-3-61; ☎ 5800 9999; |e| www.tokyo-dome.co.jp/e/; Marunouchi & Namboku lines to Kōraku-en, main exit; ¥1800-3500), is the best place to catch a ball game. It is the home ground of Japan's most popular team, the Yomiuri Giants.

Soccer

J-League soccer is currently booming in Japan. Since the country was awarded the 2002 World Cup (jointly with Korea) there's been an increased interest the game. The Japanese have decked it out with the hullabaloo of its baseball, and standards of play are rising. Tokyo only recently got its own J-League team, Tokyo Verdy 1969, which plays at the National Stadium (3, H3; Shinjuku-ku, Kasumigaoka-machi; ☎ 3403 1151; Chūō line to Sendagaya, east exit; ¥3500/1000).

Sumō

See page 27 for further information on this most Japanese of sports.

Tokyo's Home Goal

Tokyo is *the* place for front row seats at the **FIFA World Cup**, to be held from 31 May to 30 June 2002 in Japan and neighbouring South Korea. Three stadiums near Tokyo – Ibaraki, Saitama and Yokohama – will host 11 of the 32 games held in Japan.

Ibaraki is only 1hr from Tokyo on the JR Sōbu Line to Kashima-jingū station. Saitama Super Stadium is 1hr away on the Namboku line then the train to Urawa-Misano station on the new Saitama line.

The final itself will take place on 30 June at Yokohama International Stadium a mere 40min journey from downtown Tokyo. The imposing stadium, complete with giant video screens, is a short 10min walk from Shin-Yokohama or Kozukue stations. For all the latest, surf to the Japan Organizing Committee's website |e| www.jawoc.or.jp/index_e.htm.

FREE TOKYO

Tokyo is expensive, but with some imagination Tokyo offers a host of gratis attractions. These suggestions cost no more than the train ticket to get there:

Parks

Unlike Tokyo's gardens, Tokyo's parks are free, and provide a welcome escape from the urban sprawl. Try Yoyogi-kōen (p. 43) and Ueno-kōen (p. 30).

Galleries

Most private galleries don't charge admission, often because they are rented by individual artists who delight in foreign interest in their work. Ginza (p. 19) is the best place to hunt for them. Department store galleries (on upper floors) are another good bet; if not free, admission is often cheaper than museum entry fees.

Temples & Shrines

Shrines are almost always free in Tokyo and most temples only charge to enter their *honden* (main hall). *Sensō-ji* in Asakusa and *Meiji-jingū* in Harajuku are two good places to start.

Company Showrooms

OK, they're really just another form of advertising, but some showrooms in Tokyo are like small museums and they're all free. The Sony Building in Ginza (p. 19) lets you test drive all the hottest new release video games.

Markets

You can wander the world's biggest fish market, Tsukiji Shijo Wholesale Fish Market, and its great External Market for hours at no cost. Flea markets are a staple in the city and great for a roam (p. 62).

Skyscrapers

Several skyscrapers have free observation floors, eg, Tokyo Metropolitan Government Offices (p. 40) and Tokyo Big Sight (p. 33).

Nature

Plum blossoms, dearly loved as early harbingers of spring, bloom from late February to early March. Cherry blossoms arrive some time in April. A stroll in a Tokyo park on a clear spring day through a riot of blossoms is unforgettable. Look out for maple trees (during autumn foliage season, *koyō*) which go through a spectrum of yellows and oranges before climaxing in a fiery red.

David Ryan

places to stay

Finding a place to lay your head in Tokyo is easy. Finding a place that's reasonable value and fulfils your every need may not be so simple. The city's top-end and luxury hotels are world class. The staff speak English, the rooms are spotless and the service is usually impeccable. Each hotel has its own restaurants, bars and cafes. The views are some of the best. The budget accommodation is generally safe, clean and convenient. It's in the mid-range where good hotels are difficult to unearth.

Many mid-range places cater to the transient, none-too-choosy Japanese businessman and thus remain essentially adequate places to kip and not much more.

Room Rates

These categories indicate the cost per night of a standard double room. At weekends and holiday periods prices may be slightly higher.

Deluxe	¥40,000 and over
Top End	¥25,000-39,999
Mid-Range	¥12,000-24,999
Budget	¥11,999 and under

The simple task of making an international phone call from your hotel room still can be singularly difficult. Ditto paying with plastic. Japan remains a cash society at heart. Check before you check-in if you want to use a credit card.

Whatever class of hotel you're staying in, it's worth opting for a Japanese-style room. They are usually more spacious than Western-style rooms and certainly as comfortable. Above all they remind you that you're not in London or New York, or any other metropolis. The delicate smell of a straw tatami mat will stay with you long after you head home. Futons become like a second skin.

Business travellers may prefer the convenience and familiarity of regular beds, desks and in-room Internet access. But at least on your last night in town you should try a *washitsu*, a Japanese-style room.

Love Hotels

For something different, spend a night in one of Tokyo's finest love hotels. They are rented out by the hour but after 10pm the overnight rates are quite reasonable. Many adults live with their parents and share bedrooms. Love hotels are used for romantic trysts between singles but married couples also indulge. Search among the back streets of Shibuya (pictured below) – east of the station and up the hill. Select your room from the illuminated pictures in the empty foyer and pay the clerk. Ask for *tomari* or overnight rates. Rooms start at ¥7500 but the more you pay, the more exciting the decor (anything from plain to wall-to-wall Mickey Mouse).

Adina Tovy Amsel

DELUXE

Four Seasons Hotel Chinzan-sō (3, E4)
All hotels should be like this. Unquestionably Tokyo's most civilised Japanese-style accommodation, complete with ornamental ponds, gorgeous tatami rooms and all the trappings. Detractors say it's in the wilds of northern Tokyo, but actually you're much closer to the action than if you stay in Ōdaiba.
✉ Bunkyō-ku, Sekiguchi 2-10-8
☎ 3943 2222; fax 3434 5177 e www .fujita-kanko.co.jp
🚇 Yūrakuchō line to Edogawa-bashi, exit 1A
✕ 4 restaurants, bar & coffee shop ♿

Hotel Seiyō Ginza
(12, F5) Like no other hotel in Tokyo; indeed, it doesn't even feel like a hotel – more like a very wealthy friend's impossibly dignified chateau. There's no front desk, just a very discreet room with a very discreet staffer who takes care of tiresome details of your stay. Most rooms come with a personal secretary. And that's only the start.
✉ Chūō-ku, Ginza 1-11-2
☎ 3535 1111; fax 3535 1110
e sgmktng@tkf.att.ne .jp; www.seiyo-ginza .com 🚇 Ginza line to Kyōbashi, exit 2
✕ 4 restaurants, lounge bar & patisserie ♿

Hotel Sofitel Tokyo
(10, D1) It may resemble a deranged architect's graduation thesis – inverted pyramids abound – but this art-bedecked 71-room luxury hotel is one of Tokyo's finest and almost certainly its most atmospheric. It doesn't matter which room you stay in: every room's a winner with excellent views.
✉ Taito-ku, Ikenohata 2-1-48
☎ 5685 7111; fax 5685 6171
e info@sofiteltokyo .com; www.sofitel tokyo.com 🚇 Chiyoda line to Yushima, exit 1
✕ 3 restaurants ♿

Imperial Hotel (12, H3)
Gosh Jeeves, we're off to Tokyo. Better get the Imperial on the blower. One of Tokyo's grand old hotels within easy walking distance of the sights of Ginza and Hibiya-kōen. Its regulars wouldn't dream of staying anywhere else.
✉ Chiyoda-ku, Uchisaiwaichō 1-1-1
☎ 3504 1111; fax 3581 9146

Nadaman restaurant, in Tokyo's Imperial Hotel

e www.imperialhotel .co.jp
🚇 Hibiya line to Hibiya, exit 5
✕ 13 restaurants & 4 bars ♿

Park Hyatt Tokyo
(4, D1) The most breathtaking views in Tokyo can be enjoyed at this luxury hotel on the upper floors of the new 53 storey Shinjuku Park Tower. An island of luxury in the sky. Rooms are new, very stylish and complemented by some of the most impressive bars and restaurants in Tokyo. And there's a rooftop pool. Even if you don't stay here, do stop by for a drink in the Sky Bar; you'll understand why when you get there.
✉ Shinjuku-ku, Nishi-Shinjuku 3-7-1-2
☎ 5322 1234; fax 5322 1288 e www .tokyo.hyatt.com
🚊 Yamanote line to Shinjuku, west exit
✕ 3 restaurants & 2 bars ♿

TOP END

Akasaka Prince Hotel

(8, A2) Something of a landmark, both physically and socially. Much kudos is gained from saying 'I'm at the Akasaka Prince'. Rooms at this skyscraper hotel provide excellent views and spaciousness, both commodities in short supply in central Tokyo. All the top-end accoutrements are here.
✉ Chiyoda-ku, Kioi-chō 1-2
☎ 3234 1111; fax 3262 5163
🖂 akasaka@prince hotels.co.jp;www .princehotels.co.jp
🚇 Ginza & Marunouchi lines to Akasaka-mitsuke, exit D
✗ 8 restaurants ♿

Akasaka Tōkyū Hotel

(8, B2) Good value for the heart of one of Tokyo's prime business districts. This place boasts lots of good bars and restaurants scattered throughout the building, several of which are on the 14th floor, giving good views over central Tokyo. Handy transport too: the Akasaka-mitsuke subway station is in the basement.
✉ Chiyoda-ku, Nagata-chō 2-14-3 ☎ 3580 2311; fax 3592 2841
🖂 akasaka.ro@tokyu hotel.co.jp;
www.tokyuhotel .co.jp/index.html
🚇 Marunouchi & Ginza lines to Akasaka-mitsuke, exit 1
✗ 4 restaurants ♿

ANA Hotel Tokyo

(8, E4) Midway between Akasaka and Roppongi (half way between business and pleasure? Heaven and hell?), this modern 37-storey hotel is an excellent choice. It has all the amenities – fitness clubs, an outdoor pool, saunas, salons, shopping and lots of good bars and restaurants.
✉ Minato-ku, Akasaka 1-12-33
☎ 3505 1111; fax 3505 1155
🖂 www.ananet/or/jp/ anahotels/tokyo
🚇 Ginza & Namboku lines to Tameike-sannō, exit 13
✗ 8 restaurants & 4 bars ♿

Capitol Tōkyū Hotel

(8, C3) An elegant place on the same hill as Hie-jinja shrine, built around a fine Japanese garden with good restaurants and bars to take in the view. The outdoor swimming pool is a godsend in the sweltering Tokyo summer.
✉ Chiyoda-ku, Nagata-chō 2-10-3
☎ 3581 4511; fax 3581 5822
🖂 capitol.ro@tokyu hotel.co.jp;
www.tokyuhotel.co.jp/ capitol/index.html
🚇 Ginza & Namboku lines to Tameike-sannō, exit 5
✗ 4 restaurants ♿

Set sail for sound sleeps at the Hotel New Ōtani.

Bill Bachmann

Hotel Inter-Continental Tokyo Bay (3, L7)

Down on the Tokyo water-front, the Inter-Continental affects a certain European dignity served up with a characteristic Japanese attention to detail. Very elegant, but you can get the same thing nearer to the centre of town at the Imperial.

✉ Minato-ku, Daiba 1-9-1
☎ 5404 2222; fax 5404 2111
e www.interconti .com ⚑ Yamanote & Keihin-Tōhoku lines to Hamamatsuchō, south exit
🚇 Yurikamome line to Takeshiba, main exit
✗ 5 restaurants ♨

Hotel New Ōtani

(8, A1) A mega-famous hotel, renowned for the beautiful Japanese garden around which it is constructed. It has extensive shopping areas, restaurants and private meeting rooms. Yet it still feels like you're staying in a beached ocean cruise-liner. Thirty rooms on the 21st floor are reserved for women only. Yes, that's right – 34 restaurants to choose from.

✉ Chiyoda-ku, Kioi-chō 4-1
☎ 3265 1111; fax 3221 2619
e www.newotani.co.jp
🚇 Ginza & Marunouchi lines to Akasaka-mitsuke, exit 7
✗ 34 restaurants ♨

Hotel Ōkura (8, E5)

A top hotel near the US embassy that is very popular with disgraced foreign presidents, celebrities and business travellers. With a fine Japanese garden, elegant common areas and

Hilton Tokyo : a popular option for business visitors

some of Tokyo's best restaurants, there's little reason to leave its confines. Excellent business facilities.

✉ Minato-ku, Toranomon 2-10-4
☎ 3582 0111; fax 3582 3707
e www.hotelokura .co.jp 🚇 Hibiya line to Kamiyachō, exit 3
✗ 8 restaurants, 3 bars & coffee shop ♨

Keiō Plaza Intercontinental

(4, C2) It may no longer be number one in this area's top-end hotel stakes, but it's still a comfortable, well-appointed hotel that's strong on business support. Also very handy for the Tokyo Metropolitan Government Offices and the infinite distractions of Shinjuku after dusk.

✉ Shinjuku-ku, Nishi-Shinjuku 2-2-1
☎ 3344 0111; fax 3345 8269
e room-reserve @keioplaza.co.jp; www.keioplaza.co.jp
🚇 Toei Ōedo line to Tochōmae, exit A1
✗ 6 restaurants ♨

Hilton Tokyo (4, B1)

Nothing spectacular, but the excellent facilities for the business traveller on its five executive floors, including fax machines and modem lines in every room, are the big pull for this top-end place on the west side of Shinjuku.

✉ Shinjuku-ku, Nishi-Shinjuku 6-2-6
☎ 3344 5111; fax 3342 6094
e www.hilton.com
🚇 Marunouchi line to Nishi-Shinjuku, exit 2
✗ 7 restaurants ♨

Westin Hotel Tokyo

(7, D5) Modelled on a grand European hotel, with elegant common areas and classically designed rooms this is an interesting luxury option. Located in Meguro, it is removed from the more chaotic centres of Tokyo, but there's plenty of local action and Yebisu Garden Place next door.

✉ Meguro-ku, Mita 1-1-4 ☎ 5423 7000; fax 5423 7600 e www .westin.co.jp 🚇 Hibiya line to Ebisu, exit 1
⚑ Yamanote line to Ebisu, east exit ✗ 6 restaurants & 3 bars ♨

MID-RANGE

Azabu City Hotel

(3, L5) A bit on the dowdy side perhaps, but the location of this decent-value business hotel in Azabu-Jūban is a big draw, just a short train ride from Roppongi and handily placed on the Toei Ōedo subway line. You can be in Tsukiji in less than 10 minutes. Service is uneven though.

✉ Minato-ku, Azabu-jūban, 2-12-3
☎ 3453 4311; fax 5232 0435
🚇 Toei Ōedo & Namboku lines to Azabu-jūban, exit 4
✗ coffee shop

Century Southern Tower Hotel (4, D3)

Well-placed smack dab in the middle of Shinjuku, the recently built Century Southern boasts great views and, wonder of wonders, Nintendo in every room. It's quite posh, and especially good value if two share.

✉ Shinjuku-ku, Yoyogi 2-2-1
☎ 5354 0111; fax 5321 8025
🖃 www.southern tower.co.jp
🚇 Yamanote line to Shinjuku, Shin-minami exit
✗ 3 restaurants 🔧

Children's Castle Hotel (5, C5)

Great option if you're in town with the kids. The rooms are spacious and you get discount rates at the facilties of the adjoining *Kodomo no Shiro*, Children's Castle (p. 44).

✉ Shibuya-ku,

Jingū-mae 5-53-1
☎ 3797 5677; fax 3406 7805
🖃 kodomono-shiro@ post.sannet.ne.jp; www.kodomono-shiro.or.jp/hotel
🚇 Chiyoda, Ginza, & Hanzōmon lines to Omote-sandō, exit B2
✗ 1 restaurant (till 7pm) 🔧

Ginza Nikkō Hotel

(12, H4) A quality mid-range hotel in a prime location. Perfect for Izakaya-hopping, shopping and taking off at dawn to Tsukiji Shijō market. It's right on Sotobori-dōri

between Ginza and Shimbashi, a few minutes walk from Shimbashi station. The rooms here are not huge but comfortable all the same.

✉ Chūō-ku, Ginza 8-4-21
☎ 3571 4911; fax 3571 8379
🖃 yoyaku@g.nikkohtl .co.jp; www.nikkohotels .com
🚇 Ginza line to Shimbashi, exit 5
✗ 1 restaurant 🔧

Hotel Alcyone (12, G6)

A bit faded but this economical, souped-up business hotel is handily located for Tsukiji market,

Ginza is luxury central - especially when it comes to hotels.

Kabuki-za theatre and Ginza. It has 74 Western and Japanese rooms, the latter more comfortable. Soak in the large communal bath. Turn left at the Ju-nana-ju bank and it's on your left after about 100m. In terms of price it's at the bottom end of the mid-range price category.

✉ Chūō-ku, Ginza 4-14-3 ☎ 3541 3621; fax 3541 3263
📧 alcyone@minuet.plala.or.jp; www.hotel-alcyone.co.jp
🚇 Hibiya & Toei-Asakusa lines to Higashi-Ginza, exit A5
🍴 restaurant & bar

Hotel Ibis (9, C3)
Smack dab in the middle of Roppongi party-land, this reasonably-priced place is plenty used to dealing with late-night foreign revellers. Hardly the most relaxing neighbourhood to stay in, but if you stay too much, this is super-convenient.
✉ Minato-ku, Roppongi 7-14-4 ☎ 3403 4411; fax 3479 0609
📧 info@ibis-hotel.com; www.ibis-hotel.com
🚇 Hibiya line to Roppongi, exit 4A
🍴 restaurant, coffee shop & 2 bars

Roppongi Prince Hotel (9, B5)
Just about every rock hero deserving of the name has barfed, bonked, overdosed, or just plain graffitied here. It's fashionable, high-tech and boasts an outdoor heated swimming pool at its centre. The excesses of Roppongi are only 10-minutes walk

away. It is at the top end of the mid-range price category.
✉ Minato-ku, Roppongi 3-2-7 ☎ 3587 1111; fax 3587 0770
📧 rop-rsv@prince hotels.co.jp; www.prince hotels.co.jp
🚇 Hibiya line to Roppongi, exit 3
🍴 5 restaurants

Shinjuku New City Hotel (3, G1)
Rooms are slightly larger than average, but its location recommends this west Shinjuku business hotel option. It's on the quieter side of the station, handy for government offices and airport buses. Duck under the tracks and you're in full-on East Shinjuku party madness.
✉ Shinjuku-ku, Nishi-Shinjuku 4-31-1 ☎ 3375 6511; fax 3375 6535
📧 www.newcity hotel.co.jp 🚇 Toei No 12 line to Tochōmae, exit A4
🍴 2 restaurants

Tokyo Station Hotel (12, D4)
Back in 1914 some 8.9 million pieces of red brick were used to construct this now faded elegant establishment, a mere brick's throw from the Tokyo station bullet-train platforms. The rooms are nothing special, but the place still possesses a cool dignity and the location can't be beaten.
✉ Chiyoda-ku, Marunouchi 1-9-1 ☎ 3231 2511; fax 3231 3513
📧 ront@tshl.co.jp; www.tshl.co.jp
🚇 Marunouchi line to

Tokyo, Marunouchi central exit 🚉 Yamanote, Keihin Tōhoku, Sōbu, Tōkaido & Joetsū lines to Tokyo, Marunouchi central exit
🍴 3 restaurants

Trimm Harajuku (6, D2)
Trimm verging on drab perhaps, but the location of this above-average business hotel, on Meiji-dōri five minutes' walk south of Meiji-jingūmae station, can't be beaten. The rooms are a little larger than average for a mid-range hotel. The only drag is the 1am curfew for guests staying there.
✉ Shibuya-ku, Jingū-mae 6-28-6 ☎ 3498 2101; fax 3498 1777
🚇 Chiyoda line to Meiji-jingūmae, exit 4
🍴 Fujimama's (p. 76), Las Chicas (p. 77)

Yama no Ue Hilltop Hotel (3, F7)
Like something out of a 1930s Hollywood movie, this one is perched on a hill in Kanda next to the prestigious Meiji University. The hotel's brochure announces: 'Oxygen and negative ions are circulated into the rooms and its refreshing atmosphere is accepted by many, including prominent individuals, as most adequate for work and rest'. Yes indeed. A nice, dignified hotel with charm.
✉ Chiyoda-ku, Kanda-Surugadai 1-1 ☎ 3293 2311; fax 3233 4567
🚇 Chūō line to Ochanomizu, exit B1
🍴 7 restaurants

BUDGET

Asia Center of Japan
(3, J5) Good budget option in posh Aoyama that fills up quickly. Pricier rooms are worth the extra lay out, and handily boast modem lines. Exit the station under the enormous Aoyama Twin Tower bldg, turn right, and it's a short walk up the third street on the left.
⊠ Minato-ku, Akasaka 8-10-32 ☎ 3402 6111; fax 3002 0738 ℮ siacntl@blue.ocn.ne .jp ⊕ Toei Ōedo, Ginza & Hanzōmon lines to Aoyama-itchōme, exit 4 south

Hotel New Tōyō (3, C8)
Tokyo's cheapest rooms are to be found at this flophouse-turned-guesthouse in a rough-and-ready – by Japanese standards – part of town. Basic but clean Western and Japanese singles (these slightly larger) and two doubles are available. Reserve well in advance. It's two stops north of Ueno on the Hibiya line.
⊠ Taitō-ku, Nihonzutsumi 2-26-13 ☎ 3873 0343; fax 3873 1358 ℮ newkoyo@tctv.ne.jp; www.newkoyo.com ⊕ Hibiya line to Minowa, exit 3

Hotel Star Plaza Ikebukuro (2, A1)
A friendly, decent value, no-frills spot in Ikebukuro. Its handy proximity to the Yamanote line means you can be anywhere in the metropolis with 30 minutes. Apparently rooms boast 'body soup'. A nearby sister hotel is much the same.
⊠ Toshima-ku, Ikebukuro 2-10-2 ☎ 3590 0005; fax 5992 0005 ℮ www.starhotel.co.jp ⊕ Yamanote line to Ikebukuro, exit C5

Kimi Ryokan (2, A1)
Popular, clean, pleasant budget option in Ikebukuro. Book well in advance. Staff are inordinately helpful (and speak good English). Remember to inform staff if you're going to be out late.
⊠ Toshima-ku, Ikebukuro 2-36-8 ☎ 3971 3766; fax 3987 1326 ⊕ Yamanote line to Ikebukuro, west exit

Ryokan Mikawaya
(11, C3) Amiable Asakusa *minshuku*, set in an interesting working-class area, just around the corner from Sensō-ji temple. The owners are used to dealing with gaijin, and have both doubles and singles. There are communal baths for men and women.
⊠ Taitō-ku, Asakusa 1-31-11 ☎ 3843 2345; fax 3843 2348 ℮ shigetsu@roy.hi-ho.ne.jp ⊕ Ginza line to Asakusa, exit 1

Taitō Ryokan (11, C1)
Great value, helpful English speaking managers and a funky downtown location make this a winner. Can be noisy, and palatial it ain't, but who cares at this price?
⊠ Taitō-ku, Nishi-Asakusa 2-1-4 ☎ 3843 2822; fax 3843 2822 ⊕ Ginza line to Tawaramachi, exit 3

Capsule Hotels

More private, claustrophobic and coffin-sized, the capsule hotel comes with bed, reading light, TV and alarm clock. Despite their size, prices still range from ¥3500 to ¥4800, depending on the area and the facilities (also cash only). Capsule hotels are not used to hosting foreign guests or women; most of their business comes from drunken office workers who have missed the last train home. Many have a well-appointed bath area similar to a good local *sentō* (public bath).

6105

Michael Taylor

facts for the visitor

Tokyo Tower as a reference point on the Tokyo skyline.

Martin Moos

ARRIVAL & DEPARTURE

Tokyo can be reached by air from most places in the world. Direct flights are available from most European capitals, Asia, Australia, Africa and the USA. A few operators use Osaka and Fukuoka as their gateway.

Air

Tokyo's main international airport is Narita, 66km from the city. At its two terminals there are post offices, currency exchange counters, health clinics as well as restaurants and duty-free shops. Terminal 2 has showers, day rooms for napping and a children's playroom for use after arrival. A few international flights still operate through Haneda, much closer to the city centre, most notably China Airlines. International traffic is expected to increase in the future.

Narita
Left Luggage
Both Narita terminals offer left-luggage services and baggage shipping/delivery in the arrivals terminals (¥500 per item per day).

Information
General Inquiries
  ☎ 0476 34 6251
Flight Information
  ☎ 0476 34 5000
  JAL ☎ 0120 25 5971
  ANA ☎ 0120 029 222
Carpark Information
  Terminal 1 ☎ 0476 32 2253; ¥500/hr, overnight ¥3840
  Terminal 2 ☎ 0476 34 5350; ¥500/hr, overnight ¥4080
Hotel Booking Service
  Terminal 1 ☎ 0476 32 8693
  Terminal 2 ☎ 0476 34 8517

Airport Access
Train Three rail services connect Narita and Tokyo: the private Keisei line runs into Ueno (Skyliner; 1hr; ¥1920); JR Narita Express into Tokyo station (N-EX, 55mins, ¥2940) and Shinjuku (1½hrs, ¥3100); and Airport Narita *Kaisoku* (rapid train service; 1½ hrs; ¥1280) to Tokyo central. All fares are one way.

Bus Limousine Buses connect Narita with central Tokyo (1½hrs, ¥3000).

Taxi A taxi to Narita airport from Tokyo will cost about ¥30,000.

Haneda
Left Luggage
This service is located near the south exit of the monorail station (¥420 per item per day).

Information
General Inquiries
  ☎ 5757 8111
Carpark Information
  ☎ 5757 8191; ¥400/hr
Hotel Booking Service
  Arrival terminal, tour desks 3 & 5

Airport Access
Train Haneda is connected by monorail to Hamamatsuchō station on the JR Yamanote line (20mins, ¥270).

Bus Buses run between Haneda and Ikebukuro (¥1200) and Shinjuku (¥1200).

Taxi A taxi between Haneda and Tokyo station costs around ¥7000.

Bus

Domestic long-distance buses mainly arrive at Tokyo station's

Yaesu Highway Bus Terminal (12, D4; ☎ 3215 0498). Services to Osaka and Kyoto are operated by JR. Buy tickets from a Green Window office at larger JR train stations.

Train

Japan Railways' (JR) famed *shinkansen* (bullet trains) serve Northern Honshū, Central and Western Japan and Kyūshū. The slower, less expensive *tokkyū* (limited express), *kyūko* (express) and *futsū* (ordinary) are options on every route between cities however not many people use them for long distance travel. Typical one-way *shinkansen* fares are Kyoto-Tokyo ¥13,220, Fukuoka-Tokyo ¥21,210 and Osaka-Tokyo ¥13,750. The main terminals are Tokyo (3, H8) and Ueno (3, E8) stations.

Private lines running from stations on the Yamanote line are the quickest, cheapest bet to Kamakura, Mt Fuji, Hakone and Yokohama. They connect to Shinjuku (3, G2) and Shibuya stations (3, K2). The Tōbu line for Nikkō, runs from Asakusa (3, E10).

Travel Documents

Passport
If you need a visa for entry to Japan, your passport will have to be valid for three months after the date of entry.

Visa
Tourists and business visitors of many nationalities (including Australia, Canada, Ireland, New Zealand, the UK and USA) are not required to obtain visas, if staying in Japan for less than 90 days. Those who wish to stay for lengthy periods or for work or study should check with their local Japanese embassy or consulate.

Return/Onward Ticket
An onward ticket may be requested before an entry permit is granted, as well as proof of adequate funds. Usually a valid credit card is sufficient proof of funds.

Customs

There are no limits on the import of foreign or Japanese currency. Export of yen is limited to ¥5 million.

Duty Free

The limits are three 760ml bottles of alcohol, 57g of perfume, 400 cigarettes, and gifts and souvenirs up to a value of ¥200,000.

Departure Tax

The departure tax (¥2040/1020) from Narita Airport is usually included in your ticket. There is no departure tax for Haneda Airport.

GETTING AROUND

Short-term visitors and long-term residents alike mainly use the city's excellent subway system and the JR train lines, especially the Yamanote line. It rings the inner city, making anywhere accessible in under an hour. All stations have signposts and maps in English. Subway colour coding and regular English signposting make the system easy to use. The train and subway services in Tokyo are famed for their punctuality. Services are frequent and arrive on time.

Travel Passes

Short-stay visitors should get the **Tokyo Combination Ticket** day pass that can be used on all JR, subway and bus lines within the Tokyo metropolitan area. It costs ¥1580 and is available from Pass offices at major stations. Stations with Pass offices are marked with a triangle on local subway maps.

Subway

There are 13 subway lines, of which eight are TRTA lines and four are TOEI lines. The subway system is essential for getting to areas inside the loop traced by the Yamanote line. Both services are essentially the same, though ticketing is separate. Ticket vending machines that operate in English are available at every station. Services run from around 5.30am to 1am.

Bus

Although buses crisscross the city, they are difficult to use as many routes and destinations are only explained in Japanese characters. There's a flat rate of ¥200. On some routes, passengers enter at the back of the bus and pay the driver on leaving. But on most, it's pay as you enter.

Train

Tokyo is serviced by a combination of JR, private inner-city subway lines and private suburban lines. All are *gaijin* (foreigner) friendly. Most useful is the Yamanote line. Fares begin at ¥130.

Taxi

Rates start at ¥660/2km (after 11pm it's 1.5km), then the meter rises by ¥80 every 274m (every 220m or so after 11pm). You also click up about ¥80 every two minutes while you relax in a typical Tokyo traffic jam.

Taxi vacancy is indicated by a red light; a green light means there's a night-time surcharge and a yellow light means that the cab is on call. Watch out for the automatic doors on taxis. Don't slam the door shut when you get in or leave – it will magically close itself.

Car & Motorcycle

You can drive in Tokyo if you really want, but make sure you budget for subsequent psychiatric counselling. Parking space is limited and expensive, the traffic moves at glacial speed. And you'll get lost.

Major directional traffic signs are in *romaji* (using Roman alphabet) and script , but if you do decide to drive in Tokyo, a bilingual map is advisable.

Road Rules
Driving is on the left and seatbelts are compulsory.

Rental
Typical rates for small cars are ¥8000 or ¥9000 for the first day, lower on subsequent days. Mileage is usually unlimited. Car hire firms include:

Nippon Rent-a-Car	☎ 3485 7196
Dollar Rent-a-Car	☎ 3567 2818
Hertz	☎ 0120 489 882

Driving Licence & Permit
An international driving permit is essential for driving in Tokyo.

Motoring Organisations
Contact the Japan Automobile Federation, JAF (☎ 3436 245), for a copy of *Rules of the Road* before heading out.

PRACTICAL INFORMATION

Climate & When to Go

Spring, from March to May, and Autumn, September to November, are the most balmy. Typhoons usually occur in September and October. The summers are hot and humid, with temperatures getting into the high 30s. The rainy season *(tsuyu)*, in June, means several weeks of torrential rain that can play havoc with a tight travel itinerary. In winter the weather is good with mainly clear, sunny skies and the occasional snowfall. Avoid major holidays such as Golden Week (29 April to 5 May) and the mid-August O-bon festival. The city tends to close down over New Year.

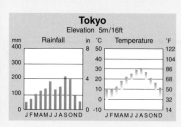

Tokyo
Elevation 5m/16ft

Tourist Information

Tourist Information Abroad

Information on Tokyo and Japan is available from the Japan National Tourist Organization (JNTO; e www .jnto.go.jp). Overseas offices of JNTO include:

Australia
Level 33, Chifley Tower, 2 Chifley Sq, Sydney, NSW 2000 (☎ 02 9232 4522, fax 02 9232 1494)

Canada
165 University Ave, Toronto, Ontario M5H 3B8 (☎ 02 416 366 7140, fax 02 416 366 4530)

UK
20 Saville Row, London (☎ 020 7734 9638, fax 020 7734 4290)

USA
Chicago: Suite 770, 401 North Michigan Ave, IL 60611 (☎ 312 222 0874, fax 312 222 0876)

Los Angeles: Suite 1611, 624 South Grand Ave, CA 90017 (☎ 213 623 1952, fax 213 623 6301)

New York: Suite 1250, One Rockefeller Plaza, NY 10020 (☎ 212 757 5640, fax 212 307 6754)

San Francisco: Suite 601, 360 Post St, CA 94108 (☎ 415 989 7140, fax 415 398 5461)

Local Tourist Information

JNTO's Tourist Information Centers (TIC) provide excellent information. They make reservations for certain hotels and *ryokan* (traditional Japanese inns). They also arrange free 'goodwill guides'.

Tokyo TIC
Chiyoda-ku, Marunouchi 3-5-1, Tokyo International Forum, B1 (12, F4; ☎ 3201 3331)

Narita Airport TIC
Terminals 1 & 2 (1, C4; ☎ 0476 34 6251)

Embassies & Consulates

Australia
Minato-ku, Mita 2-1-14 (3, L5; ☎ 5232 4111, fax 5232 4149)

Canada
Minato-ku, Akasaka 7-3-38 (3, J5; ☎ 5412 6200, fax 5412 6302)

Ireland
Chiyoda-ku, Kōjimachi 2-10-7 (3, G6; ☎ 3263 0695, fax 3265 2275)

New Zealand
Shibuya-ku, Kamiyamachō 20-40 (3, K1; ☎ 3467 2271, fax 3467 2278)

South Africa
Chiyoda-ku, Hirakawachō 7-9-2 (8, A3; ☎ 3265 3366; fax 3265 1108

UK
  Chiyoda-ku, Ichibanchō 1 (3, G6;
  ☎ 0990 61 2005, fax 5275 0346)
USA
  Minato-ku, Akasaka 1-10-5 (8, E4;
  ☎ 3224 5000)

Money

Currency

The currency in Japan is the yen
(¥). Banknotes and coins are easily
identifiable; there are ¥1, ¥5, ¥10,
¥50, ¥100 and ¥500 coins; and
¥1000, ¥2000, ¥5000 and ¥10,000
notes. The ¥1 coin is made of
lightweight aluminium; ¥5 and
¥50 coins have a hole in the middle. Recently-issued ¥500 coins
cannot be used in most vending
machines.

Travellers Cheques

There's little difference in commis-
sion charged by banks and big
hotels. All major brands are acceptable, but cheques in yen or US
dollars are preferred over other
currencies. Shinjuku's Isetan and
Keiō department stores, and
Ikebukuro's Seibu (7th floor), will
change travellers cheques.

Credit Cards

MasterCard, Visa, American
Express and Diners Club are most
widely accepted, but Japan is
predominantly a cash economy.
Top hotels and restaurants usually
accept credit cards but check first
with less exclusive places. For 24hr
card cancellations or assistance,
call:

American Express	☎ 0120 020 120
Diners Club	☎ 3797 7311
	☎ 3499 1181
JCB	☎ 3294 8111
MasterCard	☎ 0031 11 3886
Visa	☎ 5251 0633
	☎ 0120 133 173

ATMs

Scores of post offices now accept
foreign-issued cash or credit cards,
Mon-Fri 9am-5pm. Some banks and
department stores have 'Global
ATM' which accept Visa, MasterCard
and Cirrus. In Shinjuku, try the
Global ATM on the 7th floor of the
Keiō department store (4, C3); in
Ginza, in front of the Yūrakuchō
Mullion building (12, F4) next to the
Sumitomo bank.

Changing Money

Banks are open Mon-Fri, 9am-3pm,
closed national holidays. The Bank
of Tokyo's Shibuya branch (☎ 3610
7000) also has an exchange service
until 6pm.

Tipping

Tipping is not standard practice in
Japan. Expect to pay a service
charge (10-20%) at more expensive
restaurants and hotels.

Discounts

Many major sights offer discounts
for children, and very young children may be free. However don't
expect such discounts automatical-
ly as this practice still hasn't taken
off in Japan.

Student & Youth Cards

A valid international student card
will win you discounts on entry
fees to some sights in Tokyo and
sometimes discounted prices on
long-distance train travel, but
that's about it.

Seniors' Cards

Seniors can get discounts to some
major sights, and Japanese domestic
airlines (JAS, JAL and ANA) offer senior discounts of about 25% on some
flights. But the picture's essentially as
bleak as it is for youth discounts.

Travel Insurance

A policy covering theft, loss, medical expenses and compensation for cancellation or delays in your travel arrangements is highly recommended. If items are lost or stolen, make sure you get a police report straight away otherwise your insurer might not pay up.

Opening Hours

Office hours are Mon-Fri, 9am-5pm. Some businesses operate on Saturday morning. Public offices are open Mon-Fri, 9am-noon, 1-5pm. Shops are typically open Mon-Sun,10am-8pm. Major museums are open 9.30am-4.30pm. Typically, restaurants open 11.30am-2.30pm and 6-10.30pm, though there are abundant exceptions. Cheaper, family-run restaurants often stay open from 11.30am-11.30pm, particularly those around railway stations.

Public Holidays

Jan 1	New Year's Day
Jan 15	Adult's Day
Feb 11	National Foundation Day
Mar 21	Spring Equinox Day
Apr 29	Green Day
May 3	Constitution Memorial Day
May 5	Children's Day
Jul 20	Marine Day
Sept 15	Respect-for-the-Aged Day
Sept 23	Autumn Equinox Day
Oct 10	Sports Day
Nov 3	Culture Day
Nov 23	Labour Thanksgiving Day
Dec 23	Emperor's Birthday

Time

Japan is in one time zone, 9hrs ahead of Greenwich Mean Time (GMT). Daylight-saving time is not used in Japan. In train stations, bus stations and airports, a 24hr clock is used, eg 5pm is 17.00 and midnight is 24.00.

At noon in Tokyo it's:
  10pm (previous day) in New York
  7pm (previous day) in Los Angeles
  3am in London
  5am in Johannesburg
  3pm in Auckland
  1pm in Sydney

Electricity

The electric current is 100V AC (Tokyo 50 cycles, Western Japan 60 cycles). The plugs are flat with two pins, identical to those used in the US and Canadian. Equipment designed for North American 117V can be used, but a transformer is recommended.

Weights & Measures

Japan uses the metric system. See the conversion table on page 122.

Post

The government-run postal service is very reliable, and the best way to send packages and business papers overseas. You can buy stamps at most convenience stores.

Postal Rates

The basic rates for all international letters is ¥110 (over 50g, ¥190). Airmail stamps for postcards to any overseas destination cost ¥70.

Opening Hours

Most post offices open Mon-Fri 9am-5pm. Major post offices open 8am-8pm.

Telephone

Local telephone calls cost ¥70 for every 3mins. Pink phones only accept ¥10 coins. Green and grey phones accept ¥10, ¥100 coins and phonecards.

Phonecards

Phonecards are available from newsstands and convenience stores and in denominations of ¥500 and ¥1000. Lonely Planet's eKno Communication Card, specifically aimed at travellers, provides competitive international calls (avoid using it for local calls), messaging services and free email. Logon to **e** www.ekno.lonelyplanet.com for information on joining and accessing the service.

Mobile Phones

Currently Japan has the same system as North America, but not the GSM system used in the UK, Australia and the rest of Asia. Check with your service provider before you leave home that they have a roaming agreement with a local counterpart.

Country & City Codes

Japan	☎ 81
Tokyo	☎ 03
Toll free	☎ 0120

Useful Numbers

Local Directory Inquiries	☎ 104
International Directory Inquiries	☎ 0051
International Operator	☎ 0051
Reverse-Charge (collect)	☎ 0039
Time	☎ 117
Weather	☎ 177

International Direct Dial Codes

Australia	☎ 0061
Canada	☎ 001
New Zealand	☎ 0064
South Africa	☎ 0027
UK	☎ 0044
USA	☎ 001

Digital Resources

The Internet was slow in taking off in Japan, but access is rapidly improving. Some bars offer net access for free, as do some governmental and prefectural offices and computer stores.

Internet Service Providers

Most major global ISPs have dial-in nodes in Japan; it's best to download a list of the dial-in numbers before you leave home. If you access your Internet through a smaller ISP, your best option is either to open an account with a global ISP or to rely on cybercafes.

Internet Cafes

If you can't access the Internet from where you're staying, head to a cybercafe:

Click-on
   Shibuya-ku, Dōgenzaka 2-23-1, Koike Bldg 5F; (5, D2; ☎ 5489 2282; 11am-11pm; ¥500/30mins)

Manga Hiroba
   Minato-ku, Roppongi 3-14-12, Chūwa Roppongi Bldg 2F; (9, C4; ☎ 3497 1751; 24 hrs; ¥380/60mins)

Gaiax Net Cafe
   Shinjuku-ku, Nishi-Shinjuku 7-10-7, Kagaya Bldg 2F; (4, B3; ☎ 5332 9201; 10am-midnight; ¥390/30mins)

Useful Sites

The Lonely Planet Web site (**e** www.lonelyplanet.com) offers a speedy link to many of Tokyo's Web sites. Others to try include:

Tokyo English Life Line (TELLNET)
e www.tell.gol.com

Tokyo Q
e www.nokia.co.jp/tokyoq

Metropolis
e www.metropolis.co.jp

Tokyo Journal
e www.tokyo.to

Soccerphile
e www.soccerphile.com

CitySync

CitySync Tokyo, Lonely Planet's digital guide for Palm OS hand-held devices, allows quick searches, sorting and bookmarking of hundreds of Tokyo's attractions, clubs, hotels, restaurants and more – all pinpointed on scrollable street maps. Purchase or demo CitySync Tokyo at **e** www.citysync.com.

Doing Business

Kinko's, the US-based office service company offers 24-hour fax sending and receiving (and net access) at its outlets currently springing up throughout Tokyo. There are handy branches in Ueno (10, D5; ☎ 5246 9811), Kanda (13, C7; ☎ 3251 7677) and Ebisu (7, C5; ☎ 5795 1485).

Some useful business organisations are:

JETRO Business Support Center
(☎ 5562 3131; fax 5562 3100)

American Chamber of Commerce
(☎ 3436 1446)

Australian & New Zealand Chamber of Commerce
(☎ 3201 2592)

British Chamber of Commerce in Japan
(☎ 3267 1903)

Canadian Chamber of Commerce
(☎ 3224 7825)

Newspapers & Magazines

The *Japan Times, Yomiuri Daily* and *Asahi/International Herald Tribune* are English-language newspapers available at newsstands in or near train stations. *Tokyo Journal* is a good events/listings magazine sold in bookstores. *Metropolis* (formerly *Tokyo Classified*), is a free publication available every Friday from cafes and bookstores around Tokyo.

Radio

InterFM on 76.1FM broadcasts news and daily-life information mainly in English, and in seven other languages, including Spanish and Chinese.

TV

NHK is the government-run TV station. Its 7pm news is bilingual. CNN and BBC World are available in all major hotels.

Photography & Video

Print, slide film, digital memory and camera gear are easy to find in Tokyo. A 36-exposure colour print film, without processing, costs about ¥420, slide film from ¥800 to ¥980. Disposable cameras are even sold from vending machines. Processing print film is fast and economical in Tokyo. Usually a 36-exposure roll of film will cost from ¥1000 to ¥2000 to develop and print. Camera repairs are extremely expensive. Japan uses the NTSC format for video. Video cameras made in Australia and most of Europe use either PAL or SECAM tapes and these are not available in Japan.

Health

Immunisations

No immunisations are required for visitors to Japan

Precautions

Levels of hygiene in Tokyo are impeccable, and no serious health precautions are necessary.

Like anywhere else, practice the usual precautions when it comes to sex; condoms, the most popular form of contraception in Japan, are available in pharmacies and convenience stores, often in ambitious packs of 24.

Insurance & Medical Treatment

Travel insurance is advisable to cover any medical treatment you may need while in Tokyo. Medical treatment is among the best in the world, but also the most expensive. All hospitals here have English-speaking staff.

Medical Services

Hospitals with 24hr accident and emergency departments include:

Japanese Red Cross Medical Centre (*Nihon Sekijūjisha Iryō Sentā*)
(12, L4; ☎ 3400 1311) Shibuya-ku, Hiro-o 4-1-22

Saint Luke's International Hospital (*Seiroka Byōin*)
(12, J8; ☎ 3541 5151) Chūō-ku, Akashicho 9-1

Dental Services

If you chip a tooth or require emergency treatment, head to Ojima Dental Clinic (3, G5; Shinjuku-ku, Ichigaya Tamachi 2-7; ☎ 3268 8818; Mon-Fri 10am-1pm & 2-6pm).

Pharmacies

Pharmacies are easy to find and some have Japanese-English symptom charts. The American Pharmacy (12, F3; Chiyoda-ku, Yūrakuchō 1-8-1, Hibiya Park Bldg; ☎ 3271 4034) is open late and staff speak English.

Toilets

Public toilets are everywhere, but the most comfortable are in the big department stores. Japanese style toilets are the squat-down variety. Take care the contents of your pockets don't fall down them!

Safety Concerns

Chances of falling prey to crime in Japan are minimal. Pickpockets do however occasionally work crowds at festivals and in big department stores. There is a *koban* (police box) conveniently located near each train station. This is the best place for directions if lost, and the most likely place to find lost property such as wallets.

Lost Property

If you leave something behind on the train and need it back call JR trains on ☎ 3423 0111, TRTA subway on ☎ 3834 5577 and TOEI subway on ☎ 5600 2020. For property left in a taxi call ☎ 3648 0300.

Keeping Copies

Make photocopies of all your important documents, keep some with you, separate from the originals and leave a copy at home. You can also store details of documents in Lonely Planet's free online Travel Vault, password-protected and accessible worldwide. See **e** www.ekno.lonelyplanet.com.

Emergency Numbers

Ambulance	☎ 119
Fire	☎ 119
Police	☎ 110
Police (non-emergency)	☎ 3501 0110

Women Travellers

Tokyo is an extremely safe city for women travellers. Beware however of *chikan* gropers, who work rush-hour trains. If this happens grab the offending hand and shout 'Chikan!'. Violent sexual crime is rare.

Oral contraceptives *can* be found in Japan, but it is far more convenient to bring an adequate supply from home. Tampons are available but may differ slightly from those you're used to.

Gay & Lesbian Travellers

Tokyo is more hip and tolerant than its Asian counterparts when it comes to the gay and lesbian scenes. There is an active international scene that includes clubs, bars, newsletters and support groups.

Information & Organisations

The magazine *Outrageous Tokyo* lists gay-friendly associations, clubs and events. International (Gay) Friends (☎ 5693 4569; English spoken) has meetings every third Saturday of the month (IF Passport, CPO Box 180, Tokyo 100-91). Useful links are ⓔ www.lavenderlinks.com and ⓔ www.gnj.or.jp/gaynet.

Senior Travellers

There's good and bad news for seniors. Tokyo is exhausting enough if you're 21. Subways may have elevators, or their escalators may be topped with a 50-flight staircase. Age is, however, seriously respected.

Disabled Travellers

Tokyo's size and complexity make it challenging for the mobility impaired, as well as the visually and hearing impaired. Newer buildings tend to have excellent facilities. Attitudes to people with disabilities have vastly improved in the last two decades. Advanced planning is the key to a successful trip.

Information & Organisations

Get the indispensable *Accessible Tokyo* from Japanese Red Cross Language Service Volunteers (Minato-ku, Shiba Daimon 1-1-3; ☎ 3438 1311; fax 3432 5507)

Language

Although many Japanese spend years studying English, they often find communicating in it difficult. This is partly due to the techniques of language teaching used in Japanese classrooms, but it also reflects the difficulty of translation. Structurally, Japanese and English are so different that literal translations are almost

Looking good in a Tokyo traffic jam

impossible. Fortunately, getting together a repertoire of travellers' phrases in Japanese should be no trouble – the only problem may be understanding what people say back to you.

Grammar

To English speakers, Japanese language patterns often seem to be back to front and lacking in essential information. For example, where an English speaker would say 'I'm going to the shop' a Japanese speaker would say 'shop to going', omitting the subject pronoun (I) altogether and putting the verb at the end of the sentence.

Written Japanese

Japanese has one of the most complex writing systems in the world, using three different scripts (four if you include the increasingly used Roman script romaji). The most difficult of the three, for foreigners and Japanese alike, is kanji, the ideographic script developed by the Chinese. Not only do you have to learn a couple of thousand of them, but unlike Chinese many Japanese kanji have wildly variant pronunciations depending on context.

Because of the differences between Chinese grammar and Japanese grammar, kanji had to be supplemented with an alphabet of syllables, or a syllabary, known as hiragana. And there is yet another syllabary that is used largely for representing foreign-loan words such as terebi (TV) and biiru (beer); this script is known as katakana. Both syllabaries have 48 characters each, and can be learned within a week – it will take at least a month to consolidate them though.

The romaji used in this book follows the Hepburn system of romanisation.

Language Guides

If you'd like to delve deeper into the intricacies of the language, Lonely Planet's *Japanese phrasebook* offers a convenient collection of survival words and phrases for your trip to Japan, plus a section on grammar and pronunciation.

Pronunciation

One of the pluses for Westerners is that, unlike other languages in the region (Chinese, Vietnamese and Thai among others), Japanese is not tonal and the pronunciation system is fairly easy to master.

The following examples reflect British pronunciation.

a	as in 'father'
e	as in 'get'
i	as in 'pin'
o	as in 'bone', but shorter
u	as in 'flu'

Vowels appearing in this book with a macron (or bar) over them (ā, ē, ō, ū) are pronounced in the same way as standard vowels except that the sound is held twice as long. Take care with this as vowel length can change the meaning of a word, eg, *yuki* means 'snow', while *yūki* means 'bravery'. Consonants are generally pronounced as in English, with the following exceptions:

f	purse the lips and blow lightly
g	as the 'g' in 'goal' at the start of word; and nasalised as the 'ng' in 'sing' in the middle of a word
r	more like an 'l' than an 'r'

Greetings & Civilities

The title *san* is used after a name as an honorific and is the equivalent of Mr, Miss, Mrs and Ms.

Good morning.	*ohayō gozaimasu*
Good afternoon.	*konnichiwa*

Good evening.	*kombanwa*
Goodbye.	*sayōnara*
See you later.	*dewa mata*
Please/Go ahead. (when offering)	*dōzo*
Please. (when asking)	*onegai shimasu*
Thanks. (informal)	*dōmo*
Thank you.	*dōmo arigatō*
Thank you very much.	*dōmo arigatō gozaimasu*
Thanks for having me. (when leaving)	*o-sewa ni narimashita*
You're welcome.	*dō itashimashite*
No, thank you.	*iie, kekkō desu*
Excuse me/Pardon.	*sumimasen*
Excuse me. (when entering a room)	*o-jama shimasu/ shitsurei shi-masu*
I'm sorry.	*gomen nasai*
What's your name?	*o-namae wa nan desu ka?*
My name is ...	*watashi wa ... desu*
This is Mr/Mrs/Ms ...	*kochira wa ... san desu*
Pleased to meet you.	*dōzo yoroshiku*
Pleased to meet you too.	*hajimemashite, kochira koso dōzo yoroshiku*
Where are you from?	*dochira no kata desu ka?*
How are you?	*o-genki desu ka?*
Fine.	*genki desu*
Is it OK to take a photo?	*shashin o totte mo ii desu ka?*

Basics

Yes.	*hai*
No.	*iie*
No. (for indicating disagreement)	*chigaimasu*
(less emphatic)	*chotto chigaimasu*
OK.	*daijōbu (desu)/ōke*
What?	*nani?*
When?	*itsu?*
Where?	*doko?*
Who?	*dare?*

Requests

Please give me this/that.	*kore/sore o kudasai*
Please give me a (cup of tea).	*(o-cha) o kudasai*
Please wait (a while).	*(shōshō) o-machi kudasai*
Please show me the (ticket).	*(kippu) o misete kudasai*

Language Difficulties

Do you understand English/Japanese?	*eigo/nihongo wa wakarimasu ka?*
I don't understand.	*wakarimasen*
Do you speak English?	*eigo ga hanase-masu ka?*
I can't speak Japanese.	*nihongo wa dekimasen*
How do you say ... in Japanese?	*nihongo de ... wa nan to iimasu ka?*
What does ... mean?	*... wa donna imi desu ka?*
What is this called?	*kore wa nan to iimasu ka?*
Please write in Japanese/English.	*nihongo/eigo de kaite kudasai*
Please speak more slowly.	*mō chotto yukkuri itte kudasai*
Please say it again more slowly.	*mō ichidō, yukkuri itte kudasai*
What is this called?	*kore wa nan to iimasu ka?*

Getting Around

What time does the next ... leave?	*tsugi no ... wa nanji ni dema-su ka?*
What time does the next ... arrive?	*tsugi no ... wa nanji ni tsuki-masu ka?*
boat	*bōto/fune*
bus	*basu*
bus stop	*basutei*
tram	*shiden*
train	*densha*
subway	*chikatetsu*
station	*eki*
ticket	*kippu*

ticket office	*kippu uriba*
taxi	*takushii*
entrance	*iriguchi*
exit	*deguchi*
left-luggage office	*nimotsu azukarijo*
one way	*katamichi*
return	*ōfuku*
non-smoking seat	*kin-en seki*

Where is the ...?	*... wa doko desu ka?*
How much is the fare to ...?	*... made ikura desu ka?*
Does this (train, bus, etc) go to ...?	*kore wa ... e ikimasu ka?*
Is the next station ...?	*tsugi no eki wa ... desu ka?*
Please tell me when we get to ...	*... ni tsuitara oshiete kudasai*
Where is the ... exit?	*... deguchi wa doko desu ka?*
How far is it to walk?	*aruite dono kurai kakarimasu ka?*
I'd like to hire a ...	*... o karitai no desu ga*
I'd like to go to ...	*... ni ikitai desu*
Please stop here.	*koko de tomete kudasai*
How do I get to ...?	*... e wa dono yō ni ikeba ii desu ka?*
Where is this address please?	*kono jūsho wa doko desu ka?*
Could you write the address for me?	*jūsho o kaite itadake-masen ka?*
Go straight ahead.	*massugu itte*

Turn left.	*hidari e magatte*
Turn right.	*migi e magatte*

near	*chikai*
far	*tōi*

Around Town

bank	*ginkō*
embassy	*taishi-kan*
post office	*yūbin kyoku*
public telephone	*kōshū denwa*
toilet	*o-tearai/toire*
tourist office	*kankō annaijo*

What time does it open/close?	*nanji ni akimasu/ shimarimasu ka*

Signs

Information Centre	*annaijo*
Open	*eigyōchū*
Closed	*junbichū*
Toilets	*o-tearai/toire*
Men	*otoko*
Women	*onna*

Accommodation

I'm looking for a ...	*... o sagashite imasu*
hotel	*hoteru*
Japanese-style inn	*ryokan*
family-style inn	*minshiku*

Do you have any vacancies?	*aki-beya wa arimasu ka?*
I don't have a reservation.	*yoyaku wa shiteimasen*
single room	*shinguru rūmu*
double room	*daburu rūmu*
twin room	*tsuin rūmu*
How much is it per night/per person?	*ippaku/hitori ikura desu ka?*
Does it include breakfast/a meal?	*chōshoku/shokuji wa tsuite-imasu ka?*

Shopping

I'd like to buy ...	*... o kaitai desu*
How much is it?	*ikura desu ka?*
I'm just looking.	*miteiru dake desu*
It's cheap.	*yasui desu*
It's too expensive.	*taka-sugimasu*
I'll take this one.	*kore o kudasai*
Can I have a receipt?	*ryōshūsho o itadakemasen ka?*
shop	*mise*
supermarket	*sūpā*
bookshop	*honya*

Food

I'm a vegetarian.	*watashi wa bejitarian desu*
What do you recommend?	*o-susume wa nan desu ka?*

Do you have an English menu?	*eigo no menyū wa arimasu ka?*
I'd like the set menu please.	*setto menyū o onegai shimasu*
Please bring the bill.	*o-kanjō o onegai shimasu*
This is delicious.	*oishii desu*

Health

I need a doctor.	*isha ga hitsuyō desu*
How do you feel?	*kibun wa ikaga desu ka?*
I'm ill.	*kibun ga warui desu*
It hurts here.	*koko ga itai desu*
I'm allergic to (antibiotics/penicillin).	*watashi wa (kōsei-busshitsu/penishirin) arerugii desu*
I have diarrhoea.	*geri o shiteimasu*
I have a toothache.	*ha ga itamimasu*
I'm ...	*watashi wa ...*
diabetic	*tōnyōbyō desu*
epileptic	*tenkan desu*
asthmatic	*zensoku desu*
antiseptic	*shōdokuyaku*
aspirin	*asupirin*
condoms	*kondōmu*
contraceptive	*hinin yō piru*
dentist	*ha-isha*
doctor	*isha*
hospital	*byōin*
medicine	*kusuri*
pharmacy	*yakkyoku*
tampons	*tampon*
(a) cold	*kaze*
diarrhoea	*geri*
fever	*hatsunetsu*
food poisoning	*shoku chūdoku*
migraine	*henzutsū*

Time

What time is it?	*ima nanji desu ka?*
today	*kyō*
tomorrow	*ashita*
yesterday	*kinō*
morning/afternoon	*asa/hiru*

Days of the Week

Monday	*getsuyōbi*
Tuesday	*kayōbi*
Wednesday	*suiyōbi*
Thursday	*mokuyōbi*
Friday	*kinyōbi*
Saturday	*doyōbi*
Sunday	*nichiyōbi*

Numbers

0	*zero/rei*
1	*ichi*
2	*ni*
3	*san*
4	*yon/shi*
5	*go*
6	*roku*
7	*nana/shichi*
8	*hachi*
9	*kyū/ku*
10	*jū*
11	*jūichi*
12	*jūni*
13	*jūsan*
14	*jūyon/jūshi*
20	*nijū*
21	*nijūichi*
30	*sanjū*
100	*hyaku*
200	*nihyaku*
1000	*sen*
5000	*gosen*
10,000	*ichiman*
20,000	*niman*
100,000	*jūman*
one million	*hyakuman*

Emergency

Help!	*tasukete!*
Call a doctor!	*isha o yonde kudasai!*
Call the police!	*keisatsu o yonde kudasai!*
police box	*kōban*
I'm lost.	*michi ni mayoimashita*
Go away!	*hanarero!*

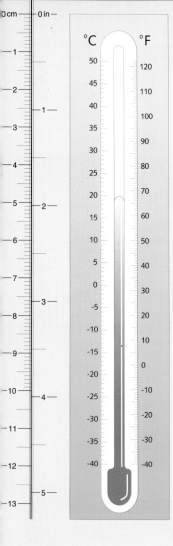

Conversion Table

Clothing Sizes

Measurements approximate only; try before you buy.

Women's Clothing

Aust/NZ	8	10	12	14	16	18
Europe	36	38	40	42	44	46
Japan	5	7	9	11	13	15
UK	8	10	12	14	16	18
USA	6	8	10	12	14	16

Women's Shoes

Aust/NZ	5	6	7	8	9	10
Europe	35	36	37	38	39	40
France only	35	36	38	39	40	42
Japan	22	23	24	25	26	27
UK	3½	4½	5½	6½	7½	8½
USA	5	6	7	8	9	10

Men's Clothing

Aust/NZ	92	96	100	104	108	112
Europe	46	48	50	52	54	56
Japan	S		M	M		L
UK	35	36	37	38	39	40
USA	35	36	37	38	39	40

Men's Shirts (Collar Sizes)

Aust/NZ	38	39	40	41	42	43
Europe	38	39	40	41	42	43
Japan	38	39	40	41	42	43
UK	15	15½	16	16½	17	17½
USA	15	15½	16	16½	17	17½

Men's Shoes

Aust/NZ	7	8	9	10	11	12
Europe	41	42	43	44½	46	47
Japan	26	27	27.5	28	29	30
UK	7	8	9	10	11	12
USA	7½	8½	9½	10½	11½	12½

Weights & Measures

Weight

1kg = 2.2lb
1lb = 0.45kg
1g = 0.04oz
1oz = 28g

Volume

1 litre = 0.26 US gallons
1 US gallon = 3.8 litres
1 litre = 0.22 imperial gallons
1 imperial gallon = 4.55 litres

Length & Distance

1 inch = 2.54cm
1cm = 0.39 inches
1m = 3.3ft = 1.1yds
1ft = 0.3m
1km = 0.62 miles
1 mile = 1.6km

lonely planet

Lonely Planet is the world's most successful independent travel information company with offices in Australia, the US, UK and France. With a reputation for comprehensive, reliable travel information, Lonely Planet is a print and electronic publishing leader, with over 650 titles and 22 series catering for travellers' individual needs.

At Lonely Planet we believe that travellers can make a positive contribution to the countries they visit – if they respect their host communities and spend their money wisely. Since 1986 a percentage of the income from books has been donated to aid and human rights projects.

www.lonelyplanet.com

For news, views and free subscriptions to print and email newsletters, and a full list of Lonely Planet titles, click on our award-winning website.

On the Town

A romantic escape to Paris or a mad shopping dash through New York City, the locals' secret bars or a city's top attractions – whether you have 24 hours to kill or months to explore, Lonely Planet's On the Town products will give you the low-down.

Condensed guides are ideal pocket guides for when time is tight. Their quick-view maps, full-colour layout and opinionated reviews help short-term visitors target the top sights and discover the very best eating, shopping and entertainment options a city has to offer.

For more indepth coverage, **City guides** offer insights into a city's character and cultural background as well as providing broad coverage of where to eat, stay and play. **CitySync**, a digital guide for your handheld unit, allows you to reference stacks of opinionated, well-researched travel information. Portable and durable **City Maps** are perfect for locating those back-street bars or hard-to-find local haunts.

'Ideal for a generation of fast movers.'

– Gourmet Traveller on Condensed guides

Condensed Guides

- Amsterdam
- Athens (May 2002)
- Barcelona (May 2002)
- Boston
- California
- Chicago
- Crete
- Dublin
- Frankfurt
- Hong Kong
- London
- New York City
- Paris
- Prague (May 2002)
- Rome
- Sydney
- Tokyo
- Venice (June 2002)
- Washington, DC (May 2002)

index

See also separate indexes for Places to Eat (p. 126), Places to Stay (p. 127), Shops (p. 127) and Sights with map references (p. 128).

PLACES TO EAT

PLACES TO STAY

SHOPS

sights quick index